The NEW THREE-LEGGED STOOL

A TAX EFFICIENT APPROACH TO RETIREMENT PLANNING

RICK RODGERS

Marketplace Books
Glenelg, Maryland

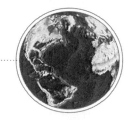

This book, along with other books, is available at discounts that make it realistic to provide it as a gift to your customers, clients, and staff. For more information on these long lasting, cost effective premiums, please call us at (800) 272-2855 or you may email us at sales@fpbooks.com.

ISBN: 1-59280-363-6
ISBN 13: 978-1-59280-363-7

Printed in the United States of America.

Contents

Introduction

The Un-Funniest Story
Ever Told

Case Study: Frank Richardson, Army veteran and business owner

In September of 2002, Frank Richardson died of natural causes in Lancaster, Pennsylvania. Frank was a good man who served four years in the United States Army and fought for his country in the Korean War. He then spent 25 years building a successful wholesale lumber business in Lancaster. Frank worked hard to improve both his own life and the lives of others around him, employing 1,000 people in the town—people like you and me who got up every morning, drank coffee, took their kids to school, built lives.

Unfortunately, Frank didn't work as hard to ensure all of his assets would be available to future generations. In general, he mistrusted financial advisors and never made time for them, a lesson he learned from watching his father follow an advisor's advice yet lose the family farm during the Depression.

Frank believed in only one financial strategy: make no changes. In keeping with this strategy, he trained the people around him to never offer him financial advice. He got his few investment tips from friends at his club and on TV. Only once did a local financial advisor get an audience with Frank, and after reviewing his retirement assets, told him he could take out a distribution and invest it in one of the mutual funds the advisor was representing. Frank politely escorted the young man to the door.

Frank avoided the subject of his retirement fund, always putting it off until later, reasoning that "they had made things way too complicated." He chose instead to help people he knew around town whom he claimed had "real" problems. Yet in focusing on the situations of others and never his own, Frank ultimately did wrong for his family.

At the time of his death, Frank Richardson was worth over $4.4 million, which included his only liquid asset—his IRA—and about $2 million in property. He left everything to his wife, Eleanor. Eleanor also trusted Frank's judgment and left the investments unchanged. Then the unthinkable happened: Eleanor died unexpectedly in 2007.

I was called in as a retirement account specialist to help settle the estate. I'd been invited by Jim Richardson, the eldest of the three surviving children. After a brief look at their records, I noticed neither Frank nor Eleanor had been taking their required minimum distributions (called RMDs for short; I discuss these throughout the book, especially in the section on How and When To Take Retirement Savings Distributions). What Frank and his wife failed to understand is the IRS has the right to levy a 50% penalty for not taking minimum distributions. The Richardson parents could have distributed over $425,000 among their children without penalty. Unfortunately, the IRS penalty was $212,500 for the missed distribution date—a date totally invented by a bureaucrat and hidden in the fine print!

I showed Jim the place in the IRS rule book where it states a husband and wife can pass an unlimited amount of assets to each other without federal estate or gift taxes. While there were no estate taxes due upon Frank's death because he left everything to Eleanor, the same didn't hold true for the estate Eleanor left to her family. Instead, the Richardson children were forced to pay an astronomical $1,035,000 federal tax on the estate (a 45% tax is levied on any amount over $2 million).

Eleanor was also a resident of Pennsylvania, which has an inheritance tax. This tax is based on to whom the money is left. Since lineal descendants in Pennsylvania are taxed at 4.5%, the state charged Eleanor's estate another $202,500 (I told you this wasn't funny!).

The final unfairness was the distribution out of the retirement account, which was taxed as ordinary income. In 2001, Congress set up the AMT (Alternative Minimum Tax), which kept the estate tax from offsetting the IRS's tax on ordinary income. The IRS subsequently charged the Richardsons $696,500 in federal income tax, even though some of the income had already been paid in estate taxes. They were essentially paying taxes on taxes!

Fortunately, Pennsylvania doesn't tax income distributed from retirement accounts, but 23 other states, like California, do. If the Richardsons had lived in California, they would've lost an additional $485,000, or 90% of everything—gone!

In the end, the Richardson siblings had to pay a total in taxes and penalties of $2,145,000—totaling 85.8% of their father's retirement account, which was worth about $2,500,000 at the time of

Eleanor's death. Because the other $2 million in assets were tied up in property, and the taxes and penalties had to be paid within nine months, they didn't have enough time to sell the properties to help with the payment. Yet if the Richardsons had had other liquid assets to pay the taxes, they wouldn't have had as much income tax to pay.

Saving everything in tax-deferred accounts like the Richardsons did is one of the biggest problems I see in retirement planning. These were good, hardworking people who had conducted themselves honorably throughout their professional lives. They paid their taxes on time, employed local townspeople in their business, and went to church. Their father's only mistake was in not understanding the IRS's basic distribution rules—rules even a first year financial planning student would have known. Of course, the Richardson children were mad as could be and wanted to take the IRS to court, but what was done, was done.

Rest assured, what I just described is a true story—and not the exception to the rule. A kind heart and an empty head won't stand up in a court of law. Your protection is knowledge. You can either get it from me or someone like me in your own town, but whatever or whomever the source, you need to know your options.

What could the Richardsons have done differently? For starters, a simple action such as a properly drawn will would've provided for the establishment of a credit shelter trust upon Frank's death. When Frank died in 2002, $1 million of property could have been set aside in a credit shelter trust and not been exposed to tax ($1 million was the maximum amount that could avoid estate tax in 2002). The income would have continued to be paid to Eleanor, but this would have removed $1 million from her estate. This step would have saved $360,000 in federal estate taxes alone.

Next, Eleanor should have taken out the RMDs from the retirement account each year; had she done so, she would have saved the $212,500 in tax penalties. She could have put her savings into a passive investment plan (I'll talk more about this in "Leg Two" of the book) and possibly made a comfortable annual return. For example, if the amount she saved in taxes lost to penalties had found its way into an investment program earning merely 5%, this would provide additional income of $10,625 per year.

As Eleanor didn't need her distribution income, she could have gifted some or all of her distributions to her children and grandchildren (gifts can currently be made for up to $13,000 per year to as many people as you want without being subject to gift tax). Had she gifted away the entire minimum distributions each year, she would have saved an additional $225,000 in estate tax. Add that to the investment program, and the annual income would have increased to $21,875 (of course, that amount would have been taxed, but we'll also discuss more about investments and taxes in Leg Two).

Finally, Eleanor should have rolled over Frank's retirement account to her name and named her children as beneficiaries. This would have allowed each child to take minimum distributions over their lifetimes, delaying the payment of income tax until the money was actually withdrawn from the account each year.

These are easy steps that could have reduced the total federal, inheritance, and income taxes on Frank's IRA to $800,000, or 32%—a whole lot better than 85.8%! Getting this advice from a financial planner would likely have cost him less than $1,000 for a few hours of the planner's time. Even if it cost him $10,000, his family still would have saved over a million dollars—dollars that are now going to fund government programs, most of which won't even benefit the great state of Pennsylvania where Frank and Eleanor made their home.

 With this book, my goal is to help you retain as much of your hard-earned retirement assets as possible—and to avoid the heartbreaking outcome experienced by the Richardson family. The Three-Legged Stool™ approach to financial security makes it both easy to understand how to achieve this retirement security and difficult to "lose balance"—that is, to get off-track once you've established your plan.

The book is divided into three main sections representing each of the three "legs," or components, you will need to have the most tax-effective financial structure.

- **Leg One—Tax-Deferred Savings Strategies.** This section covers how to make the most of your IRA, 401(k), and other tax-deferred retirement vehicles.

- **Leg Two—After-Tax Savings Strategies.** In this section, I discuss how to build your investment plan around the important concept of asset allocation; five important risk-reducing investment strategies; and—last but not least—how to structure your investments in the most tax-efficient way possible.

- **Leg Three—Tax-Free Savings Strategies.** This section focuses on the smartest tax-free retirement savings methods—the Roth IRA and Roth 401(k)—and how to convert your existing accounts to these fantastic options.

After learning about these three key factors in retirement savings, we'll wrap up the book with discussions about the all important Retirement Distribution (R/D) Factor™ and how it factors into your eventual retirement savings distributions; a closer look at

Social Security; and a special bonus section on estate planning. Be sure to keep an eye out for plenty of my quick tips along the way, as well as the list of recommendations I include at the end of each section.

It's easy for anyone to believe the government protects its citizens' rights. But the truth is, in matters of taxes, once the IRS gets its hands on your money, you can kiss that money goodbye. You must act before that event takes place—and this book will help you do it. At the end of the day, it's what you and your family get to keep that counts.

The tax code is governed by a group of bureaucrats who have no concern for what's fair and what's not. Their job is simple: get as much of your money as they can legally tax. My office phone number is 717-560-3800; I'd love to hear from you.

WHY WOULD THE IRS STEAL YOUR MONEY?

After reading the terrible story about the Richardsons above, you're probably asking yourself: *What possible motive could the IRS have for stealing my retirement money?*

The answer is simple and straightforward: our government is going to need your money—and lots of other Americans'—to keep our country running.

As of March 2009, our country's national debt totaled more than $10.9 trillion (and the number continues to rise by $1 million every minute!). That amounts to $55,700 of debt for each adult in the United States. Yet this is a mere drop in the proverbial bucket compared to what the government will owe in benefits to Social Security and Medicare recipients far into the future, as well as in pensions to military and civilian government workers.

In other words, the *true* liability of the United States isn't only the Treasury bills, notes, and bonds we sell to finance our annual deficit and keep the country running, but it's also all of the promises we've made to make benefits payments in the future. Plus, we have many new governmental departments such as Homeland Security to be funded, not to mention two wars and the Army, Navy, and Marine Corps budget shortfalls. All told, our government's debt list of projects, departments, agencies, bureaus, and programs is a mile long. And where do you think the Treasury is going to get its funding? From YOU!

Imagine it is April 15th. At the last minute, you drop off your tax forms at your local post office. You're one of a hundred people lined up outside the post office, and you assume everybody is there for the same purpose—to pay taxes. But you're wrong: forty of those folks (people with lower incomes) will be excused from paying any income taxes, while twenty people (the middle class) will pay merely a token amount. *It's the 40 remaining in line (the upper-middle class, like you) who shoulder nearly all of the taxes.*

That's right. Forty percent of Americans pay 100% of the tax bills.[1] And guess what? It's not enough! In view of this statistic, it's easier to see the IRS' motive for wanting to take as much of your retirement money as possible.

At this point, you may be thinking: *But I'm not wealthy.* Sorry—it doesn't take a lot to be rich in the eyes of the IRS. Simply having your name on an IRA or 401(k) plan distribution list makes you a target. The IRS sees a huge amount of collective dollars—$47 trillion, to be exact—stashed away in IRAs and retirement programs. This has caused it to become extremely aggressive in taxing those

---

1   *The Wall Street Journal*, "The Taxpaying Minority," April 16, 2007, sec. 1, p. A15.

assets. So you may not like it, but believe me, it's true—the IRS has a big red bull's-eye painted on your retirement plan.

Our individual state governments also have a hand out. Why? Because they have been losing money for many of the same reasons the country has—and the largest revenue losses are about to occur as the baby-boom generation retires and states begin to face the higher costs (and other issues) associated with that retirement[2]. For instance, costs for state pensions and retiree health insurance will increase as the baby boomers age. States will bear a particularly heavy burden for health care for the aging population, as it is the states' Medicaid programs (rather than federally run Medicare) that pay for long-term care. The significant revenue losses these budget proposals will engender will make it still more difficult for states to meet these responsibilities.

I know it's not fair, but we have little control over it. What each of us *does* have control over is taking the right steps toward protecting retirement assets from unfair taxes—taxes you may not even know you owe!

WHO AM I TO GIVE YOU ADVICE?

My job as both a financial advisor and the author of *How to Stop the IRS from Stealing 75% of Your Retirement* is to provide asset protection solutions that truly work. My many years of success in doing this job have been recognized throughout the industry: In July 2007, *Wealth Manager* magazine named my company, Rodgers & Associates, one of the country's top wealth managers for the fifth consecutive year. The magazine's ranking is based on the asset value of each participating wealth manager's aver-

---

2   The first members of the baby-boom generation are now turning 60 at a rate of 7,900 a day, or a whopping 330 every hour.

age client relationship as of December 31, 2006, and is calculated by dividing the total client assets under management by the total number of client relationships. Rodgers & Associates was one of only four firms named from Central Pennsylvania and ranked as wealth managers.

If you need more to go on than an endorsement from one of the nation's foremost wealth management publications, don't worry, because I'm going to tell you how you can test my ideas yourself. You'll be able to do this by following the very specific course of action I lay out in the pages of this book. It won't be a general approach to the game of beating the IRS; developing a solid asset protection plan isn't like a tennis match, for instance, where your strategy might be "play aggressively" or "play safe shots." Rather, the following sections will give you a defined set of choices to make for every possible circumstance that might arise.

THE THREE-LEGGED STOOL™ APPROACH TO FINANCIAL SECURITY

Imagine you're playing a game called Retirement Distribution. Your opponent, the IRS, wrote the rules of the game. The secret to winning this game is to keep the IRS out of your financial affairs before they have the *right* to interfere. My role in the game is to explain the fine print in the rule book and to provide you with a strategy that covers all eventualities, so in the end, you win and the IRS loses.

As I mentioned earlier, this book focuses on three strategies that can help you emerge victorious when facing a formidable opponent like the IRS. I'd like to go into a bit more detail about each of the three strategies now.

Tax-Deferred Savings Strategies™

This leg of my Three-Legged Stool™ Approach to Financial Security is comprised of 401(k) accounts, traditional IRA accounts, and annuities. The main benefit of this leg is to help with income taxes while you're still working. It's the easiest money to save, because you're realizing an immediate tax benefit when you put money into one of these account types. Tax-deferred savings are also easier to invest in because the earnings are tax-deferred as well, so you can invest in these financial instruments that generate income without concerning yourself with an immediate tax liability.

401(k) contributions may be made through payroll deductions, and most people never miss the money since it's automatically taken out of their net pay by their employers before they ever receive their paychecks. IRA contributions are also easy to make for those seeking a last-minute tax deduction before their filing deadline. For these reasons, tax-deferred savings are usually the largest portion of a person's savings. It's not unusual to see someone entering retirement with all of their financial assets in tax-deferred savings accounts.

The major problem with relying only on this scenario is every dollar a retiree spends will be taxable when he or she reaches for it. For example, a retiree who wants to spend $100,000 from savings is going to need to take out $134,000 to net $100,000 after-tax. Note also that tax law changes over the past several years have left many people ineligible to make a deductible IRA contribution. Those who are eligible can usually save a couple hundred dollars on their income taxes when making a contribution.

In addition, tax-deferred accounts come with penalties for drawing the money out before retirement age. Most employer plans will only allow early withdrawals in cases of extreme hardship.

After-Tax Savings Strategies™

This leg is comprised of your bank and brokerage accounts, investment real estate—anything that isn't a retirement account. It's harder to save in these accounts because the money is taxed before you receive it. You must also be careful of how it's invested, because the investment return will be taxed along the way.

The benefit of after-tax savings doesn't come until you're already retired. When you want to spend $100,000 from your after-tax savings, there will be very little tax liability. What tax liability there is will most likely come from long-term capital gains, which currently has a maximum tax rate of 15%.

The biggest danger with after-tax savings isn't tax issues but accessibility. Because the money has already been taxed and there are usually no penalties to access it, it's the first place a person goes to get money. Funds that were originally earmarked for retirement can easily be spent on vacation homes, cars, college, etc. This is why many people end up with only tax-deferred savings at retirement. They've already spent the after-tax savings on other things along the way.

Tax-Free Savings Strategies™

The final leg of the Three-Legged Stool™ Approach includes funds such as Roth IRAs and Roth 401(k)s. These fund types have no immediate tax benefits. Instead, the real benefits come at retirement, since money withdrawn from a Roth IRA or Roth 401(k) after you turn age 59½ is tax-free. When you want to spend $100,000 of your Roth IRA/401(k) money after you retire, you simply pull those funds from your Roth, and the tax liability is zero!

In light of this, you might wonder why everyone doesn't save for retirement in a Roth IRA/401(k). A big reason is because unlike tax-deferred savings, Roth IRA/401(k)s offer no immediate tax benefits, so it's harder to save money because it's done with after-tax dollars. A taxpayer left with the choice of putting money into a tax-deductible IRA or a Roth IRA will often choose the former because he or she will see an immediate return in tax savings.

The bigger problem for the Roth is getting money into it. The IRS limits who can contribute to a Roth IRA, based upon income. A taxpayer can only contribute the maximum to a Roth if his Modified Adjusted Gross Income (MAGI) is below $99,000 for a single filer or $156,000 for joint filers. In addition, Roth 401(k)s only started a couple years ago, so not many employers are offering them at this time.

***

The remainder of this book is dedicated to exploring each of these three critical topics in more detail, so you can enter retirement with a balanced three-legged stool. In the next section, Leg One, we'll start our discussion of the first topic with a refresher course on the bread and butter of retirement plans: the tax-deferred savings account.

The NEW THREE-LEGGED STOOL

Chapter 1

Leg One: Tax-Deferred Savings Strategies

THE MAIN TAX-DEFERRED ACCOUNTS: A REFRESHER COURSE

The term *tax-deferred* refers to the postponement of paying taxes on earnings until a later date. There are many ways to defer taxes; rather than spend time on all of them, I'll focus this section on using retirement accounts for tax deferral.

Tax-deferred retirement accounts allow employees to save money in the present, dealing with taxes in the future. To take advantage of tax-deferred savings, an employee can choose to place pre-tax dollars, up to a certain amount, in various retirement accounts. These dollars aren't taxed when you place them in the account— they're only taxed when you withdraw them from the account.

Rick's Tip

The best part about saving money in tax-deferred retirement accounts is you lower your current taxable income—and may be able to benefit from taxation at a lower tax bracket.

The two main types of retirement accounts are individual and employer sponsored. Let's take a closer look at these two types.

Individual Retirement Plans

Individual retirement plans are those that can be purchased without an employer. Primary examples include the individual retirement account (IRA) and solo 401(k). Two other types of individual accounts—Simplified Employee Pension (SEP) IRAs, and Savings Incentive Match Plan for Employees (SIMPLE) IRAs—may also function as employer sponsored plans.

Individual Retirement Account (IRA)

An IRA (Individual Retirement Account) is a personal retirement account that provides income tax advantages to individuals saving money for retirement. Since the objective of creating the IRA is to assist taxpayers in providing for their retirement, tax law levies penalties on withdrawals taken before retirement age of 59½. Tax law in the area of early withdrawals is complex. The typical tax penalty is 10% of the amount withdrawn prior to age 59½, unless certain exceptions apply. You should seek professional advice whenever you need to make significant withdrawals prior to age 59½, since many times you can avoid the penalty with proper planning.

You usually must begin taking money from your IRA no later than April 1 of the calendar year following the date you reached age 70½. The rules established by the government regarding these required minimum distributions (RMDs), their timing, the amounts, the recalculations, and the effect various beneficiary designations have on them are among the most complex of the Internal Revenue Code. For failing to take timely withdrawals, the penalty is 50% of the shortfall between what you should have withdrawn and the amounts you actually withdrew by the proper date. This punitive penalty is matched only by the civil fraud penalty in severity. The necessary calculations are therefore not something that most individuals should attempt on their own.

Contributions to IRAs

You can make deposits/contributions to an IRA each year up to the amounts allowable under the tax law. The contribution or deferred limits of an IRA plan are $5,000 in 2009. Employees age 50 or older can contribute another $1,000. An income tax deduction may be available for the tax year for which the funds are deposited. The principal and earnings on these deposits aren't taxed until you withdraw the money from the account. Withdrawals from an IRA may be subject to income taxation in the year in which you take them.

Solo 401(k)

A solo 401(k) plan works just like a regular 401(k) plan combined with a profit-sharing plan (see the next section on Employer Sponsored Retirement Plans for more on 401(k)s and profit-sharing plans). The difference is a solo 401(k) can only be implemented by self-employed individuals or small business owners who have no other full-time employees (the exception is if your full-time employee is your spouse). If you have any other full-time employees age 21 or older, or part-time employees who work more than 1,000 hours a year, you need to include them in any plan you set up, which negates your ability to adopt a solo 401(k) plan.

Contributions to Solo 401(k)s

In 2009, contribution limits to solo 401(k)s are $16,500. An additional $5,500 may be contributed by employees age 50 or older.

Simplified Employee Pension Individual Retirement Account (SEP) IRAs

A SEP IRA is a type of retirement plan an employer with less than 25 employees can establish, including self-employed individuals with no employees. SEP IRAs are adopted by sole proprietors or small business owners to provide retirement benefits for themselves and, if they have any, their employees. The benefits of this approach are there are no significant administration costs for a self-employed person with no employees, and the employer is allowed a tax deduction for contributions made to the SEP plan. The employer makes contributions to each eligible employee's SEP IRA on a discretionary basis. If the self-employed person does have employees, all employees must receive the same benefits under a SEP plan. Since SEP accounts are treated as IRAs, funds can be invested the same way as any other IRA.

Contributions to SEP IRAs

SEP IRA contributions are treated as part of a profit-sharing plan. Contributions are tax-deductible, and the employer can contribute up to 25% of an employee's net compensation, or $49,000, for 2009 (indexed annually for inflation). Only the employee's first $245,000 in gross compensation is subject to the employer's contribution rate. Employers aren't required to make annual contributions; however, if they do make annual contributions, all eligible employees must receive those contributions. Contributions may be made to the plan up until the date the employer's tax return is due for that year.

When a business is a sole proprietorship, the employee/owner both pays themselves wages and makes a SEP contribution that's limited to 25% of wages, which are profits minus SEP contribution. For a particular contribution rate (CR), the reduced rate is

CR/(1+CR); for a 25% contribution rate, this yields a 20% reduced rate. Thus the overall contribution limit (barring limits) is 20% of 92.935225% (which equals 18.587045%) of net profit.

Participants can withdraw the money at age 59½; prior to that, there's a 10% penalty or exercise tax. Distributions are taxable as ordinary income in the year they're received.

Savings Incentive Match Plan for Employees (SIMPLE) IRAs

The SIMPLE IRA is a type of employer-provided retirement plan available to an "eligible employer"— an employer with no more than 100 employees. An employer who has already established a SIMPLE IRA may continue to be eligible for two years after crossing the 100 employee limit. Self-employed workers with no employees also are eligible to establish these accounts.

The SIMPLE IRA is an employer sponsored plan, like more well-known plans such as the 401(k) and 403(b) I describe in the next section. The SIMPLE IRA is an attractive plan for employers because it doesn't incur many of the administrative fees and paperwork of plans such as the 401(k). Employers also benefit from the tax-deductible contributions to the plan. Employees may elect to have salary deferrals to contribute to the plan like the 401(k). Assets inside of SIMPLE IRAs can be invested like any other IRAs in stocks, bonds, mutual funds, bank deposits, etc.

Contributions to SIMPLE IRAs

Like a 401(k) plan, the SIMPLE IRA is funded by a pre-tax salary reduction, and, like other salary reduction contributions, these deductions are subject to ordinary taxes including Social Security, Medicare, and federal unemployment tax (FUTA). Contribution limits for SIMPLE plans are lower than for most other types of employer-provided retirement plans: $11,500 for 2009, as compared to $16,500 for conventionally defined contribution plans. Employees age 50 or older can contribute a catch-up amount of $2,500.

Rick's Tip

If the whole topic of Social Security has you scratching your head, don't worry: I go into plenty of detail about this complex system and its associated taxes in the upcoming Understanding Social Security section.

With SIMPLE IRAs, the employer has the option of matching the employee's deferrals up to 3% of the annual salary or making non-elective contributions of 2% or less to all eligible employees. In both cases, the employer's contributions can't exceed $8,000 a year.

While the employer may pick the financial institution in which to deposit the SIMPLE IRA funds, employees have the right to transfer the funds to another financial institution of their choice without cost or penalty. Distributions from SIMPLE IRAs follow the same rules as regular IRAs, with one exception: if premature distributions are taken before the employee reaches age 59½, and during the first two years after the employee starts participating in the plan, the penalty is 25%, not the usual 10%. Withdrawals are fully taxable at regular income tax rates, and mandatory withdrawals must begin at age 70½. A SIMPLE IRA account can be rolled over into a traditional IRA tax-free after the first two years.

Employer Sponsored Retirement Plans

Employer sponsored accounts are only available to employees of the business offering them. Employer sponsored plans fall under one of two areas—defined benefit and defined contribution plans.

The most common type of defined benefit plan is the pension, while the most common type of defined contribution plans are the 401(k), 403(b), and 457 plans. The Simplified Employee Pension (SEP) IRAs and Savings Incentive Match Plan for Employees (SIMPLE) IRAs I described above may also fall under this category for employers with limited numbers of employees.

Defined Benefit (Pension) Plans

A defined benefit plan is commonly referred to as a pension. A pension is a steady income given to a retiree typically in the form of a guaranteed monthly annuity. The formula for calculating the amount of pension income a retiree will receive is usually based on a combination of service and salary. For example, a pension formula would state that the employee earns 1½% for each year worked (the service portion) times their average earnings for the last five years (salary portion). A retiree with average earnings of $100,000 and 30 years of service would receive a pension of $45,000 per year.

Defined Contribution Plans

A defined contribution plan provides an individual account for each participant. The benefit received by the retiree is based solely on the amount contributed to the account plus earnings on the funds invested. The contribution formula is usually based on salary only and could be a fixed percentage each year, or varied depending on the profits of the company. When the company chooses to tie the amount of the contribution to their profits, the plan is referred to as a "profit-sharing" plan. When the contribution is based on a fixed percentage, it's called a "money purchase" plan. Upon retirement, the employee's account is used to provide retirement benefits, which can be paid in a variety of ways, such as through the purchase of an annuity, to provide a regular monthly income.

In the past couple of decades, defined contribution plans have grown rapidly and are now replacing traditional defined benefit plans as the primary retirement savings account for most employees. This change has shifted greater responsibility for retirement income from employers to individuals. Future benefits from these accounts depend on the level of contributions from the employee and employer during their careers.

401(k) Plans

The most common type of defined contribution plan is the 401(k). Under Section 401(k) of the Internal Revenue Code, enacted in 1978, employer and employee contributions to tax-deferred retirement accounts are excluded from wages subject to the federal income tax. Earnings within the accounts are tax-deferred until they are withdrawn, when the money is taxed as ordinary income. In the Economic Growth and Tax Relief Reconciliation Act (EGTRRA) of 2001, Congress raised the maximum allowable contributions to defined contribution plans, and proposals for further increases will likely remain on the legislative agenda. There are also restrictions on how and when employees can withdraw these assets, and penalties may apply if the amount is withdrawn while an employee is under the retirement age as defined by the plan.

The way most 401(k) plans work is the employee elects to have a portion of his or her wage paid directly, or deferred, into his or her 401(k) account. The employee can select from a number of investment options where she wants contributions invested. Most employers offer an assortment of mutual funds that emphasize stocks, bonds, money markets, or the company's stock.

Rick's Tip

One of the best features of the 401(k) plan is some employers will opt to match the employees' contribution: as a defined contribution plan, the amount the participant gets in retirement is based on the amount contributed to the plan and investment returns on those contributions.

Contributions to 401(k) Plans. The process for making contributions to 401(k) plans involves employees making periodic contributions from their paychecks before taxes. Any investment earnings or additional amounts matched by the company are also tax-deferred until retirement. The contribution or deferred limits of a 401(k) plan are $16,500 in 2009. Employees age 50 or older can contribute another $5,500.

Employers that offer matching contributions usually base the amount on what the employee contributes. This matching contribution is often 25%, 50% or even 100% up to a maximum level set by the employer. It's best for employees to contribute at least as much as the employer is willing to match to take advantage of this valuable employee benefit.

403(b) Plans

The 403(b) is a tax-deferred retirement plan available to employees of educational institutions and certain non-profit organizations as determined by section 501(c)(3) of the Internal Revenue Code. The company determines further eligibility based on an employee's salary and status (for example, full-time versus part-time). The 403(b) plan has many of the same characteristics and benefits of a 401(k). Contributions can grow tax-deferred until withdrawal, at which time the money is taxed as ordinary income.

Contributions to 403(b) Plans. The annual contribution limits for 403(b)s are the same as 401(k)s—$16,500 in 2009, and employees age 50 or older can contribute another $5,500. An additional catch-up provision may be available to employees age 50 or above. This increase is known as the 15-year rule, a special provision that increases the elective deferral limit by as much as $3,000 more than the current $16,500 limit (as of 2009). To qualify, an employee must have completed at least 15 years of service with the same employer (years of service need not be consecutive) and can not have contributed more than an average of $5,000 to a 403(b) in previous years. The increase in the elective deferral limit can't exceed $3,000 per year under this provision, up to a $15,000 lifetime maximum.

Employees get to choose where their money is to be invested from among the plan providers offered by employers. The providers offer different investment options, but employers aren't responsible for administrating the plans. 403(b) plan providers primarily offer annuities and some mutual funds. The annuities can be either fixed or variable. As with all annuities, gains aren't taxed until the participant starts receiving distributions.

457 Plans

A 457 plan is a tax-exempt, deferred compensation program made available to employees of state and federal governments and agencies. The 457 plan is similar to a 401(k) plan, except there are never employer matching contributions and the IRS doesn't consider it a qualified retirement plan. The other key difference: there's no 10% penalty for withdrawal before the age of 59½. However, the withdrawal is subject to ordinary income taxation.

Participants can defer some of their annual income, and contributions and earnings are tax-deferred until withdrawal. Distributions start at retirement age but participants can also take distributions if they change jobs or in certain emergencies. Participants can choose to take distributions as a lump sum, annual installments, or as an annuity. Distributions are subject to ordinary income taxes and the amounts can not be transferred into an IRA.

Contributions to 457 Plans. An employee can contribute $16,500 for 2009 into a 457 plan. The 457 plan allows for two types of catch-up provisions. The first is for employees over age 50, who can contribute a catch-up amount of $5,500 into their governmental 457 (catch-up contributions are not provided for non-governmental 457 plans). The second, which is also available only to governmental 457 plans, is much more complicated and can be elected instead by an employee who is within three years of normal retirement age. This second catch-up option is equal to the full employee deferral limit or another $16,500 for 2009. The second type of catch-up provision is limited to unused deferral limits from previous years. An employee who had deferred the maximum amount of money into the 457 plan every year they were employed previously would not be able to utilize this extra catch-up.

Rick's Tip

Though governmental 457 plans may be rolled into other types of retirement plans—including IRAs—non-governmental 457 plans can only be rolled into another non-governmental 457 plan.

PREVENT THE IRS FROM TOUCHING TAX-DEFERRED DISTRIBUTIONS

In the first part of Leg One, we talked about the primary kinds of tax-deferred savings strategies, which include IRAs, pensions,

401(k)s, and many other plans. One of the biggest decisions you'll face when you retire is how to start tapping into these plans. At that point, the money you've been saving tax-free all throughout your career will finally be subjected to taxes. Your challenge will be to prevent the IRS from taking too much of your distributions in taxes.

There are three types of distribution options: annuity, lump sum, and partial lump sum. The Department of Labor requires that all plans must offer an annuity payment. However, not all plans are required to offer lump sum or partial lump sum. Hopefully your employer will allow you to choose between the three, though some employer plans only allow annuity payments.

Annuity Payments

All employer plans are required to offer you an annuity payout in the form of monthly income. These payments will continue for the rest of your life (in the case of your 401(k), you can surrender the balance to an insurance company that will guarantee payments for life; the amount of monthly payment will depend on the balance in the account and your age). When considering early retirement, the annuity payouts will be smaller, because you have a longer life expectancy. The payments are taxed as ordinary income and don't qualify for any special tax treatment for federal income tax purposes. Some states tax these payments, and others don't.

Rick's Tip

Alabama, Hawaii, Illinois, Mississippi, and Pennsylvania don't tax pensions. Alaska, Florida, Nevada, South Dakota, Texas, and Washington have no state income tax. All other states may tax all or part of your pension income.

In most cases, annuity payments aren't eligible to be rolled over (transferred) to an IRA. Rolling over distributions from an employer plan to an IRA avoids taxation. The one exception is if the annuity payouts are for a period of less than ten years. Note a ten-year payout isn't less than ten years. I had a client, Mark Johnson, who learned this lesson the hard way.

Case Study: Mark Johnson, retiree

Mark was a retiree who'd elected a ten-year payout of his pension, since they didn't offer a lump sum distribution at the company he retired from. He'd been retired for three years when he started doing some consulting work. Since he didn't need the pension income, he put the payments into his IRA and called it a rollover. But the IRS doesn't allow these payouts to be rolled over, because the period elected wasn't less than ten years.

We had to pull out all of the contributions Mark made and the earnings. The excess contributions were subject to a 15% penalty. His tax returns needed to be amended for the years he didn't claim the pension income, and he had to pay back taxes with interest. The IRS could have charged a penalty for the back taxes but chose not to, because we caught the mistake and corrected it voluntarily. But the mistake was costly enough as it was.

 The moral of this story is: When you're asked to choose a payout option for your annuity upon retirement, choose wisely! With most retirement plans, this is an irrevocable decision.

Payout options vary among plans, but the following choices are the most frequently offered:

- **Life Income:** This option will provide an income for as long as you live; however, the pension dies with you. So while life income will give you the maximum monthly income available, there are *no* benefits available to your heirs.

- **Joint and Last Survivor (J&LS):** With this option, you'll receive a pension for life and provide a survivor income for the life of your spouse. This survivor income will usually represent a percentage of your pension income, typically anywhere from 50-100%. But keep in mind your monthly pension will be reduced when you add a beneficiary. The greater the benefit to the beneficiary, the *smaller* your pension income will be to you.

- **Life Income with Guarantee:** This option will also provide you with an income for the rest of your life; however, if you die before the end of the guarantee period, the remaining payments left in this period will be paid to your beneficiary. For example: If you died in the 8th year of a 20-year guarantee, 12 years of payments would be paid to your beneficiary. The guarantee periods generally range from 5-20 years. Note, not all pensions have a guarantee clause; they must only offer the life or joint life options. The concern of some retirees is that they elect the life option and then pass away after only receiving a few payments with nothing going to their heirs. The guarantee period is to assure that the heirs will receive something if the retiree passes away soon after beginning distributions.

- **Joint and Last Survivor (J&LS) with Guarantee Period:** With this option, you may add a guarantee like the one I described above to your J&LS pension. This is an important consideration if you and your spouse want to be sure there's money payable to your estate in the event of both of your premature deaths.

- **Income Drawdown:** This option is a variation on the other choices. Here, the pension administrator calculates the present value of what your payments will be over your life expectancy and shows this amount as a lump sum. Each time you receive a payment, this lump sum is reduced until it reaches zero. If you were to die before the lump sum is exhausted, the balance would be paid to your beneficiary.

Though there are a range of annuity payment options available, this approach still has flexibility problems. Let's say, for example, you choose the J&LS option. Your monthly payment is reduced to cover your spouse if you're the first to die. What happens if your spouse dies before you? You won't need the survivor protection any more, but the payment won't revert to the higher amount. You'll be paying for a survivor benefit you no longer need for the rest of your life. Even if you were to remarry, you can't add your new spouse as beneficiary.

Inflation creates another problem for most annuity payments in the private sector. Government pensions usually offer cost of living adjustments (COLA), though they're not always automatic. Retiring at age 65 with a $3,000 per month pension may be a comfortable income today, but that amount will have the purchasing power of only $1,500 per month in 20 years at an inflation rate of just 3.5%. Your standard of living would erode significantly if you didn't have any other savings to supplement your income.

Finally, when you submit your pension paperwork, you're making a decision that will have to last 20 to 30 years. Are you ready to make that kind of decision when you retire? I can't tell you how many people have sat in my office at retirement and said, "Rick, I'm finally retired, and I'm not going to work another day in my life!" Yet a year later, many of those same people say, "Rick, I'm sick and tired of painting the house. I need something to keep my mind occupied. I've decided to do some consulting work for my former employer a couple days a week." Those people no longer need the same pension income, but they can't turn it off, and they end up paying tax on it every year because the payments aren't eligible for rollover.

Lump Sum Payments

If you decide to take a lump sum distribution of your entire balance from all of your employer's qualified plans (pension, profit-sharing, or stock bonus plans), you have one year from the date of your retirement to complete the transaction.

Once you indicate your choice, you'll be asked whether you plan to roll it over to an IRA or not. If you choose *not* to roll it over to an IRA, the employer is required to withhold 20% for taxes. All of the investment earnings and pre-tax contributions will be subject to income tax. You'll also be subject to a 10% early withdrawal penalty if you are not age 55 or older.

There are several advantages to choosing a lump sum payout. Rolling it over directly to an IRA avoids the 20% withholding and allows the money to continue to grow tax-deferred until you decide to draw it out. You can roll it over to an IRA and then start taking monthly distributions. If you use the inflation-fighting investments I describe in Leg Two, you can increase that amount each year to keep pace with inflation. The payments can be stopped or modified if you decide to do some consulting work.

You can also take out a lump sum amount if you want to make a down payment on a vacation home or other big purchase. Your IRA allows you to name a beneficiary who will receive the balance in the account when you die. You can name multiple beneficiaries and change them whenever you want. Finally, if you decide later you'd rather have a guaranteed monthly income, you can use the lump sum from your IRA to buy an annuity with the balance in your account.

If your employer offers both after-tax and pre-tax retirement options, you'll be glad to know the EGTRRA I described earlier liberalized the rules regarding the permissible movement (portability) of assets between eligible retirement plans. The changes to these rules now allow you to roll over after-tax assets from your company plan to your IRA.

The benefit of rolling over the after-tax assets is that the earnings continue to grow tax-deferred in your IRA. The drawback is you will be responsible for keeping track of the after-tax assets in your IRA by filing a form 8606 with your tax return each year you make contributions or withdrawals. This may be desirable if you're going to implement the Roth strategy I describe in Leg Three. If not, you'll want to elect to receive the after-tax contributions in a separate check so they aren't commingled in your IRA.

Rick's Tip

Note many employers who offer both pre-tax and after-tax retirement options commingle the two in one overall retirement plan statement. The administrator for your qualified plan is ultimately responsible for keeping track of which portion of your balance is attributed to after-tax and pre-tax assets. However, it helps if you check your statements periodically to ensure the tabulations match what you think they should be. This will allow you to clarify possible discrepancies with the plan administrator.

If you're holding any money in your retirement account in company stock, you'll need to elect how that money is to be distributed. See the next section titled NUAs Prevent the IRS from Pilfering Retirement Fund Deposits for a full discussion on this topic.

Let's look at the two options side by side.

Table 1.1 - Lump Sum vs. Annuity		
	Lump Sum	Annuity
Money for Survivors	Yes	Only a spouse at time of election (payment is reduced if spouse is covered)
Inflation Hedge (COLA)	Yes	Rarely Offered (Payment is reduced if COLA elected)
Flexible Income Payments	Yes	No
Investment Control	Yes	No

As you can see, when you're given the option of either an annuity or a lump sum payout, you should choose the latter for its overall flexibility and advantages.

Partial Lump Sum (PLS) Payments

Some public employee pension plans offer retirees a combination of lump sum and annuity payments, which is generally referred to as a partial lump sum (PLS) option. This option allows retirees to receive a portion of their retirement benefit as a one-time payment in exchange for a permanently reduced monthly annuity payment. The PLS payment will reduce the account balance used to calculate the annuity payment dollar for dollar. Reducing the account balance by taking a PLS won't affect the length of time the monthly annuity benefit is payable.

Most plans require the PLS to be between defined minimum and maximum amounts. For example, the plan may stipulate the payment can't be less than six times or more than 36 times the monthly amount that would be payable under the plan of payment selected. The maximum amount could also be worded in a way that the lump sum payment can't result in a monthly benefit that's less than 50% of the original monthly benefit. The total amount paid as lump sum and monthly payments will be equal to the amount that would have been paid had the retiree not elected to receive a lump-sum payment.

As a lump-sum distribution, the PLS is fully taxable and subject to the other rules connected to a full lump-sum distribution.

Tax Alternatives to the IRA Rollover

In the previous sections, we talked about the benefits of rolling over your retirement account distributions to an IRA. While doing this will allow you to avoid the tax man for awhile longer, you may be interested in exploring other options that force you to pay the IRS piper up front, but could be better suited to your situation.

Ten-Year Averaging

In order to qualify for ten-year averaging, you must meet the following criteria:

- If the employee has more than one account in any category, all of these accounts must be distributed as a lump sum distribution in a single tax year.
- You can not have previously used ten-year averaging for figuring tax on a lump sum distribution.
- You participated in the plan for at least five years prior to the tax year of lump sum distribution.

- The plan was a tax qualified plan under the tax law.
- You were born before January 1, 1936.

If you meet the above tax tests, the lump sum distribution you report on your tax return may qualify for special tax treatment that includes the ten-year averaging tax option. This doesn't mean you get to pay one-tenth of the tax each year for the next ten years. Rather, you pay the entire tax in one year, but the tax is calculated as if it had been received over ten years. If you want to consider this option, be sure to consult a tax professional who's experienced with this calculation to help you through the process.

Capital Gains

The 20% capital gains tax election can be made to compute the tax on the taxable part of the lump sum distribution that applies to the portion received for participating in the plan before 1974. This choice allows taxpayers who were born before 1936 to have the pre-1974 taxable portion taxed on their tax return at a 20% tax rate, and the rest of the lump sum distribution, including the portion for all post-1974 participation, taxed as ordinary income using the ten-year averaging tax option.

Ordinary Income

A lump sum (and PLS) distribution will be subject to ordinary income tax in the year you receive it. Payments made to the retiring employee directly from an employer plan are subject to the mandatory withholding of 20% federal tax, but this doesn't necessarily mean it's taxed at 20%. If you receive a large distribution in one tax year, it could easily put you in the highest tax bracket of 35%.

Rick's Tip

Let's look at some case studies to explore the thought process that goes into deciding which distribution method is best in a given situation. I want to stress how important it is to *think through these options and get counsel before making your election.* You only have one chance to make these elections, and the implications are significant. I have people coming into my office all the time with a retirement mess, and I ask them why they made the choices they did. Most of the time, I find they just followed what someone else had done who'd retired before them. Yet the circumstances of each retiree are unique. You want to make the right choice for *you,* and that choice may be something completely different than what a coworker did.

Case Study: Jonas Beiler, former military officer and retiree

Jonas Beiler had several careers during his working lifetime and was preparing to retire from a company he'd worked with for the past ten years. Jonas retired earlier from the military and was already receiving a pension from the Navy. He'd accumulated $300,000 in his 401(k) and wanted to take it as a lump sum and use the proceeds to pay off the mortgage on a property in Florida that he bought a few years earlier. He and his wife Sarah planned to split their time between Pennsylvania and Florida during their retirement. The Beilers came to me for help with figuring out how to meet these goals.

We determined between Jonas' Navy pension, Social Security, and the couple's other savings, they wouldn't need this $300,000 to meet future income needs. Jonas was born before January 1, 1936, so he qualified for ten-year averaging. The money had all been put into the account in the last ten years, so none of it was eligible for capital gains treatment. Jonas could take the money out as a lump sum and pay ordinary income tax on the distribution, or he could apply ten-year averaging. Let's look at the difference between the two options:

- Ordinary income tax: $100,770
- Ten-year Averaging: $64,475

The other option was to try to spread the distribution over more than one tax year. That would disqualify the distribution for ten-year averaging treatment. The tax under ten-year averaging treatment was so favorable it made for an easy decision.

Case Study: Victor Goldman, consultant and retiree

Victor was age 55 and was leaving his current position to start a consulting business on his own. He already had clients who wanted to use his services, and he estimated he'd be able to comfortably provide for his income needs from his consulting income for ten years into the future. His 401(k) was worth $500,000, and he sought my advice about whether he should take it as a lump sum and pay the tax right then, since he was 55 and not subject to a 10% penalty, or if he should rollover the money to an IRA and pay the tax later.

Victor's options:

- Direct Transfer Rollover @ 8% return = $1,079,460 in ten years
- Income distributed with 20% withheld for tax = $69,080 per year
- Lump Sum Distribution with 20% withheld for tax @ 6.4% after-tax return = $743,830 in ten years
- After-tax income distributed = $47,600 per year

Income tax rates would have had to increase dramatically in the next ten years for the strategy to favor taking the lump sum right then. Even if Victor would have qualified for ten-year averaging, paying the tax right then would have been a significant disadvantage he wouldn't have been able to overcome within a ten-year time frame. Since he didn't need to use all the money then, he elected the direct transfer rollover.

Case Study: Dave Mills, engineer

Dave was a former engineer who always prided himself on thoroughly researching a topic and making informed decisions. When he retired from a local farm equipment company, he decided to make all of his retirement decisions on his own, since he'd always done his own investing and had grown his 401(k) to $1 million. Unfortunately, he made a $200,000 mistake simply by failing to check the right box on his Request for Distribution form.

Since Dave neglected to check the rollover box, his employer thought Dave's retirement money was coming directly out of its plan, which made it subject to the 20% mandatory withholding. So Dave's employer withheld 20% for taxes and sent him a check for the difference. Dave called his employer immediately after he received the check, but it was too late—the employer had already sent the $200,000 to the IRS, since employers are required to submit taxes withheld within 24 hours if the amount exceeds $100,000. The IRS literally got its money before Dave did, and Dave then called me seeking help on how to fix his mistake.

Dave could have simply rolled the remaining $800,000 over to an IRA and been done with it. But look at the consequences of that choice:

Distribution Amount	$1,000,000
20% Withholding	($200,000)
	=======
Net Check Received	$800,000
Tax on $200,000	($50,000)
Penalty if under age 55	($20,000)
Lost earnings on $200,000	($12,000)
Total Shrinkage	($82,000)

Another alternative would have been for Dave to come up with $200,000 from his personal funds so he could roll the whole $1 million over to the IRA. But not many people have an extra $200,000 lying around, including Dave. However, he did have a home worth $500,000 that had a mortgage balance of $100,000.

We arranged for a home equity line of credit so he could borrow $200,000 from his home and subsequently rollover the entire $1

Rick's Tip

If you aren't sure how to fill out the rollover paperwork, by all means, get help! In order for the distribution to be a direct rollover, the proceeds must be made payable to the custodian for benefit of you. Sometimes the check goes directly to the custodian. Other employer plans make the check payable to the custodian but send it to the employee. Either way is acceptable. But beware—if you receive your check and it's 20% light, you made a mistake, and the 60-day clock is ticking! You'll only have 60 days to figure out a way to make the best of the situation.

You should also be careful if you're rolling over company stock. You'll want to read the next section on NUAs to determine if you want to rollover the stock or take it in kind. If you decide to rollover the stock to an IRA, make sure it's a custodian that can accept stock. I highly recommend you consult with a financial advisor who's experienced with handling rollovers with company stock. The tax laws involving company stock rollovers are very complicated; I typically see a 50% error rate with rollovers involving company stock in some form. Most of the mistakes can't be fixed, and the tax consequences are high.

For example, I've seen cases were the employee took the company stock out of the plan and replaced it with cash so he could say the entire amount was rolled over. This isn't permitted! The consequences involve an excess contribution penalty on the cash contribution. The cash contribution must be removed from the IRA and tax paid on any earnings as well as on the stock distribution. The stock distribution will also be subject to penalty for not being reported as a taxable distribution.

million within the 60 day limit required for such transactions. When he filed his taxes the following year, he recouped the $200,000 that was withheld and paid back the line of credit. He had to pay the bank interest on the $200,000 he borrowed—but the IRS didn't pay Dave a dime on his $200,000 they held onto for a year.

To avoid making Dave's mistake yourself, you can elect a direct rollover to an IRA. The direct rollover won't be subject to 20% mandatory withholding. The rollover will still be reported to the IRS as a distribution, but it will be coded as a rollover on the 1099-R, a tax reporting document similar to the 1099-DIV brokerage firms use to report dividend income. You'll need to show the amount on your tax return for the year the money was distributed, but it will appear as a rollover and therefore won't be taxed.

Dave may also have been able to avoid his mistake if he'd simply left his retirement in his 401(k) plan, which some employers allow. There are good reasons to consider doing this. If you're not retiring but rather are going to work for another employer that has a 401(k), it's likely your new employer allows rollovers from other plans—so you could roll the money from your old plan directly into the new employer's plan. And if you're between ages 55 and 59½, withdrawals from an employer plan aren't subject to the same 10% IRS penalty you'd incur if you withdrew your money from an IRA during that same period. You must wait until age 59½ to withdraw penalty-free from an IRA.

On the other hand, the main problem with leaving the money in your employer's plan is the employer has control over it. It's your money, but the plan administrator has to sign off on distributions. What would happen if the employer went out of business? Another one of my clients, Marie Hawgood, found out.

Case Study: Marie Hawgood, executive

Marie worked for a small company in Massachusetts that had a 401(k) plan with T. Rowe Price mutual funds. When she left the company to move to Pennsylvania, she left her 401(k) in place because she liked the T. Rowe Price funds and didn't need the money. The account was small, and over the years, she received quarterly statements indicating the funds were performing well. She made periodic changes online among the funds that were offered through the plan and was able to grow the account to $100,000 by the time she was ready to retire.

When Marie eventually tried to rollover the account to her IRA, she found she needed the administrator's signature to distribute the account—yet the company she had worked for was no longer in business. She came to me for help after six frustrating months of trying to get T. Rowe Price to release her own money. They weren't disputing the fact the funds belonged to Marie; instead, they were disputing she didn't have the authority to distribute them. Can you imagine?

We obtained a copy of the plan documents and were eventually able to track down one of the signers of the plan at his new job. Once the forms were properly signed, T. Rowe Price released the funds, and Marie rolled them over to her IRA. This was difficult enough with Marie on hand to help. I've helped with even more complex situations were the account owner was deceased, and we had to try to get the funds released to the beneficiary. In at least one instance, the dispute took two years to resolve. By then, we'd missed the deadline for electing distributions over the beneficiary's lifetime and were forced to distribute the account. The moral of this story: when in doubt, roll over your company plan to an IRA where you're in control of the funds!

Case Study: Harry Thompson, retiree

The costs of mistakes are not always tax related, as another one of my clients, Harry Thompson, discovered. Harry had been employed at Armstrong World Industries for over 30 years. He retired with a good pension and had accumulated $800,000 in the company's 401(k) plan, $500,000 of which was in Armstrong stock. Armstrong stock had had a pretty good run and was trading at around $80 a share. Harry thought the stock should soon reach a high and wanted to be able to sell it quickly. He didn't like the method used to sell the stock when it was in the 401(k), so he decided to roll it over to an IRA so he'd have more control. He'd recently received a flyer from his insurance agent that said the agent could handle IRA rollovers, so he rolled over his whole 401(k) to an annuity through the agent.

What this agent (who'd never done a rollover involving stock) failed to tell Harry was an annuity can't accept stock. Any stock would need to be sold before attempting the rollover. So when Harry's first post-rollover statement arrived in the mail, it showed the $300,000 in non-stock deposits but the $500,000 in Armstrong stock didn't show anywhere, despite the fact his last 401(k) statement showed everything leaving the account. In the meantime, Armstrong stock hit $90 per share and then started coming down. After months of getting the runaround from the insurance company about the whereabouts of the stock, Harry came to me in frustration to get the rollover completed.

We tried to get the rollover reversed, but the annuity had a 7% penalty on the $300,000, and the "free look" period had already passed. This meant the $300,000 had to stay put with the insurance company, or else the company would help itself to $21,000 of the money. We finally tracked the stock down through the transfer agent. It had been registered to the insurance company as custodian for Harry's IRA. Once we knew where the certificate was, it was a simple matter to get the shares reissued. We set up an IRA account with a discount broker and had the shares reissued to the discount broker as custodian for Harry. Harry ended up with two IRAs—one with the insurance company and another with a discount broker and his company stock. They were both reported as rollovers, so there were no tax problems to deal with. The problem was the Armstrong stock had fallen to $50 per share, and the account was now worth $300,000. Harry had missed his opportunity to get out of the stock when it was trading at $90 per share.

Another detail of Harry's situation is he had a pension from Armstrong that wasn't eligible for rollover. He needed to decide whether to take a survivor benefit for his wife, Jean. Jean didn't have a pension of her own, and after evaluating their other resources, we determined Harry needed to provide a survivor benefit. The

Rick's Tip

The strategy I referenced in the last paragraph of my case study about Harry Thompson is called pension maximization. I've found this strategy only works in about half of cases—mainly because most people aren't in good enough health at retirement to qualify for preferred rates. However, it's great when it works, since it addresses the problem of Jean passing away first. In this case, Harry could let the policy expire since he wouldn't need it any longer. Or, if he remarried, he could change the beneficiary to his new wife so she'd be covered. This wouldn't be an option with the pension. In Harry's case, both he and Jean had more income than taking the 50% survivor option.

annuity would pay $3,000 per month with no benefit or $2,500 per month with a 50% survivor benefit. If Harry were to die, Jean would receive $1,250 per month.

Harry was 59 years old and in good health. We were able to find a life insurance company that would write a policy on Harry's life that would pay Jean $2,500 per month if Harry were to die. The premium on this policy was $450 per month. After qualifying for the policy and the stated premium, Harry elected the $3,000 per month pension with no survivor benefit. He used $450 of the pension income to pay the premium, which left him with a net income of $2,550 per month.

Penalties

From the case studies above, it's clear you should avoid expensive consequences of improperly handling your retirement assets. It's bad enough you have to pay income taxes on withdrawals without also incurring penalties. Some of these penalties are well known, while others aren't. Let's review some of the common transactions and mistakes that could result in IRS penalties on your IRA assets or IRA-related transactions.

Early-Distribution Penalty

If you're under age 59½ when a distribution occurs from your IRA, you may have to pay a 10% early-distribution penalty on the gross distribution amount. There are several exceptions to the 10% early-distribution penalty that are discussed throughout this book, primarily in the upcoming section on early retirement. Qualifying for one of these (or any other) exceptions can often be handled properly when the IRA custodian/trustee reports the distribution as one that meets an exception. Improper reporting could result in the need for you to pay penalties you could have avoided.

Tax on Excess Contributions

Each year, there's a maximum limit on the amount you may contribute to an IRA. In 2009, the limit is $5,000, or $6,000 if you're age 50 or older. Contributions in excess of the limit are referred to as "excess contributions," and they must be removed plus any earnings by your tax-filing deadline (including extensions) for the year. Failure to do so will result in a 6% tax assessment on the excess amount for each year the excess remains in the IRA. The excess tax applies to any amount that's contributed to an IRA that shouldn't be, such as the examples above with the retiree who attempted to roll over his pension payments or the person trying to take out company stock and replacing it with cash. This excess tax penalty can become a substantial amount, and failure to remove the excess amount in a timely manner could result in double taxation of the assets.

Excess-Accumulation Tax

IRA owners must begin taking required minimum distributions (RMDs) from their IRAs for the year they reach age 70½, and they must continue to distribute a minimum amount from the IRA each subsequent year. There's a 50% penalty for failing to distribute the RMD amount. For example, if your RMD for this last year was $10,000 and you distributed only $5,000 from your IRA, you'll owe the IRS $2,500 (50% of $5,000) plus tax on the entire $10,000.

Rodgers' Recommendations for Preventing the IRS from Touching Tax-Deferred Distributions

All employers are required to offer an annuity option for distributing your company retirement, but not all require you to take it. Elect the lump sum when offered. You can always convert the lump sum to annuity payments on your own at a later time.

Be careful when electing your distribution using the company forms. Mistakes can result in lost investment earnings and significant tax penalties. Consult a retirement planner to help you evaluate which options are best for you and complete the paperwork properly.

If you do make a mistake with your retirement distribution, get help quickly. There's only a 60-day window to fix rollover mistakes.

Consult a retirement planner who's experienced with handling company stock in a retirement plan. Mistakes are costly, and you don't want to miss an opportunity that may have been available to you.

You may not always have been able to avoid paying income taxes, but you can avoid paying penalties. You don't want to suffer avoidable penalties and taxation on any retirement transactions. Make sure you're familiar with the various restrictions on contributions and distributions. Be sure to consult your tax professional regarding transactions that could result in penalties.

Your coworker may know more than you do about financial matters, but his choices aren't necessarily the best ones to make for everyone. Consider your distribution options carefully in light of your own unique situation.

NUAS KEEP THE IRS AWAY FROM TAX-DEFERRED STOCK DISTRIBUTIONS

I want to begin this section with a story about a client of mine, Rodney Hartwell, whose stock distributions from his tax-deferred retirement plan weren't structured in the most tax-efficient way possible.

Case Study: Rodney Hartwell, medical supply executive

Rodney Hartwell, an executive at a medical supply company, was planning on retiring at year's end. Rodney had $100,000 worth of employer's stock held in the company's 401(k) plan with a cost basis of $20,000. A local investment advisor recommended Rodney roll his company stock into a low-cost IRA, explaining the advantages of the IRA and telling Rodney his account would grow larger because the tax would be deferred—and there was also the likelihood of potential returns with the hot mutual fund he just happened to be recommending for the IRA.

The advice this investment advisor gave to Rodney wasn't unusual, since tax-deferred savings accounts are most people's go-to method of saving for retirement. But as I mentioned in the last section, the major problem with this scenario is every dollar a retiree wants to spend is going to be taxable when he or she reaches for it.

The advisor likely failed to explain this unfortunate fact to Rodney, and so when his IRA eventually began to distribute income, that income was taxed at ordinary income rates on his $20,000 cost basis and could eventually have been taxed even higher (35%) on his $80,000 gain.

Rick's Tip

Note the NUA distribution must be taken as a lump sum distribution, not a partial lump sum distribution, and in order to qualify for a lump sum distribution, the employee must take the distribution all within the same calendar year.

The advisor should have recommended Rodney use an often-overlooked tax strategy known as net unrealized appreciation (NUA). How does an NUA work? Here's an example. An employee is about to retire and qualifies for a lump sum distribution from a qualified retirement plan. He elects to use the NUA strategy, receives the stock, and pays ordinary income tax on the average cost basis, which represents the original cost of the shares. This strategy allows the tax to be deferred on any appreciation that accrues from the time the stock is distributed until it's finally sold.

The NUA strategy would have allowed Rodney to receive an in-kind distribution of his company's stock and pay income tax only on the average cost basis of the shares, rather than on the current market value. In that case, Hartwell's tax on the $80,000 gain would be treated as long-term capital gains and taxed at a maximum of 15%, resulting in a potential tax savings of $12,000.[1]

Five Steps to a Successful NUA Transaction

Before exercising a distribution or rollover, follow these five steps designed to help you understand what it takes to complete a successful NUA transaction.

---

1 Of course, the $20,000 basis would be taxed as ordinary income.

1. Start early—the NUA transaction may take several weeks. You should be sure to obtain a written copy of your cost basis before initiating the rollover. You can get the formal documentation of the cost basis of the company stock; you can also request formal documentation showing your employer's promise to make an in-kind distribution of the company shares.

2. Determine the amount of gain in the stock price. In an employer-sponsored retirement plan, you can elect an NUA on some, all, or none of the shares. Note, however, on shares you bought for more than the current stock price, it's not logical to elect this strategy. Instead, seek out shares that are currently selling for twice your cost basis.

3. Select the sequence of transactions when the plan holds other assets in addition to employer securities. You can transfer the company stock portion (which still qualifies for the tax break on the NUA) to a taxable (non-IRA) brokerage account, and you can roll the non-company stock portion of the plan into an IRA rollover account. You should execute the IRA rollover first for all assets except the company stock, then the NUA shares can be distributed in-kind, with nothing to withhold for the IRS from either transaction. Note that unless it's a trustee-to-trustee transfer, or if the only remaining asset being distributed is employer stock, your employer should withhold 20% of distributions from a qualified plan for taxes.

4. Know your liabilities. You should have your tax professional prepare a tax projection to determine the amount needed, and be prepared to pay the tax man in April.

5. Prepare an exit strategy. Assuming you're optimistic about your company's future and proceed with the in-kind distribution, you should still have an exit strategy if the stock starts to decline.

Rick's Tip

A few words of caution before you jump on the NUA band-wagon: first, an NUA distribution may not be a good idea if the company's outlook is bleak. The tax benefits are wasted if the company stock declines significantly after the distribution. An investor with 98% of his retirement account tied up in one stock may want to consider liquidating a portion of his stock position and distributing a smaller portion of the stock in-kind. Second, never ask for in-kind distributions of company stock in December. It's better to wait until the beginning of the next year, because the entire distribution (rollover and in-kind distribution) must be completed in the same calendar year.

One possibility would be to give some or all of the stock to a charitable remainder unitrust (CRUT). Once the stock is transferred to a CRUT, the shares can be sold by the trustee and reinvested in a diversified portfolio that can provide lifelong income to the donor. The charitable deduction might even offset most of the tax obligation on the cost basis.

Rodgers' Recommendations for NUAs

- If you own large quantities of company stock inside a retirement plan, you should know about Net Unrealized Appreciation (NUA).

- NUA allows the tax to be deferred on any appreciation that accrues from the time the stock is distributed until it's finally sold.

- Distributions must be taken as lump sum distributions, *not* partial lump sum distributions.

- In order to qualify for the NUA treatment, an employee must complete the entire distribution within the same calendar year.

✳ ✳ ✳

With the tax-deferred savings strategies I've covered in Leg One now under your belt, you can get started on creating the all-important tax-deferred part of your retirement savings plan. However, don't forget a well-rounded retirement plan includes more than just tax-deferred strategies; it must also include after-tax strategies, which I'll tell you about in greater detail in Leg Two.

Chapter 2

Leg Two: After-Tax Savings Strategies

TRANSFER HIGHLY TAXED ASSETS INTO TAX-DEFERRED ACCOUNTS

To recap, the after-tax savings strategies leg of my three-legged stool approach is made up of your bank and brokerage accounts, investment real estate—basically, anything that's not a tax-deferred retirement account. After-tax savings strategies have become more prevalent in the face of the growing recognition that we don't live in a tax-free environment.

As a result, we've had to re-craft our tools in order to devise innovative new strategies that can keep the IRS from taxing our retirement. For example, I've found for typical mutual funds on an after-tax basis, turnover was the real killer. That's why I now use asset classes for my clients and lengthen the holding period, allowing them to grow on a compounding basis, then I reinvest the earnings. If you do this, your money will grow at a faster rate. Remember, it's not how much you earn, it's how much you keep!

I want to tell you a story about another retiree, Shirley Bachman, to help illustrate the importance of including after-tax strategies in your retirement plan.

Case Study: Shirley Bachman, retiree

Shirley Bachman was a widow who had accumulated what she thought would be a comfortable savings for retirement. Her financial assets totaled $1 million, and it was split nearly equally between an IRA and a taxable account. She counted on the income from her investment accounts, Social Security, and a small pension to make ends meet.

When Shirley turned 70½, she had to begin to take her required minimum distribution (RMD) from her IRA, and the additional taxable income was making 85% of her Social Security taxable. She found making the higher quarterly estimated tax payments was straining her budget. What she needed was a more tax-efficient way to generate income.

Shirley lived in a single family home she'd raised her children in and didn't really want to move. However, she was considering the option of selling her home and moving into a smaller condominium that would hopefully be less costly to maintain.

When Shirley came to me for financial advice, I found she considered herself to be a moderate investor. She knew growth would be needed to help keep pace with inflation. Her accounts were invested equally in stocks and bonds. Like most Americans, she had invested both her taxable account and IRA the same way. Could there have been a better way to allocate the investments from a tax-efficient standpoint and still maintain the moderate risk allocation?

The answer was yes—an answer supported by a study from Robert Dammon and Chester Spatt, finance professors at Carnegie Mellon. Dammon and Spatt published a study in the *Journal of*

Finance[1] that showed some simple rules of thumb. Their first assertion was that investors should put their taxable fixed income investments (government bonds, corporate bonds, and certificates of deposit), along with real estate investment trusts (which are mostly taxed at ordinary income tax rates) into tax-deferred accounts. Ordinary income tax rates can be as high as 35%, but long-term capital gains and qualified dividends are taxed at a maximum rate of 15%, so the stock assets should be placed in taxable accounts. The study found this allocation was beneficial even for those who trade stocks frequently.

Thus, putting the most highly taxed assets into tax-deferred accounts like an IRA or 401(k), and holding those with tax preferred treatment like stocks and stock mutual funds, which generate long-term capital gains and qualified dividends, can easily add 20% in portfolio value over time. This is especially true for middle-aged investors who have a longer period to compound.

Rick's Tip

Note that calculating taxes can get complicated because it depends on how long you hold the security and whether the accounts will be subject to state income tax.

Some investors would argue that it doesn't matter if you hold bonds in a taxable account, because they'd only invest in tax-free municipal bonds. Dammon and Spatt's study concluded municipal bonds should only be used in taxable accounts after the tax-deferred accounts have been filled with taxable bonds. The reason is, municipals historically pay a much lower yield than taxable bonds. Earning

---

1   Robert M. Dammon, Chester S. Spatt, and Harold H. Zhang. "Optimal Asset Location and Allocation with Taxable and Tax-Deferred Investing," *Journal of Finance 59*, no. 3 (June 2004): 999-1038.

the higher returns on the taxable bonds in a tax-deferred account more than offsets the tax paid when you have to start drawing from those accounts and paying tax on the distributions.

The disadvantage is compounded if you end up holding stocks in the tax-deferred account, because you're holding municipal bonds in the taxable account. You lose the 15% tax treatment on your capital gains and dividends, because all withdrawals from tax-deferred accounts are taxed as ordinary income. The investor could end up paying as high as 35% on the capital gains earned from his or her stock holdings in an IRA.

Paying the lower tax rates on stocks is just one advantage of holding them in a taxable account. The other comes from the reality that not every stock investment is going to work out favorably. Every portfolio is going to have some losers from time to time. Taking a loss in a taxable account allows you to write off that loss against other income. Capital losses will offset capital gains 1 to 1. In the event you have a net loss, you can write it off against other income up to $3,000 in one tax year. Losses over $3,000 can be carried forward to future tax years until they can be used. Losses in a tax-deferred account can't be used on your tax return.

The argument we frequently hear against this strategy surrounds the need for a lump sum withdrawal when the stock market is down. What if you need to take out $50,000 in the middle of a stock market correction? Wouldn't you be putting yourself in a situation where you bought high and are now selling low? Shouldn't you keep some money in bonds in the taxable account for this situation? Not at all. The objective in this situation isn't to reduce your stock holdings in a down market.

To accomplish this, we'd sell $50,000 of the stock security in the taxable account and simultaneously sell $50,000 of a bond in the tax-deferred account. With the proceeds from the bond sale, we'd buy $50,000 of the same security. You've effectively taken your withdrawal from the bond side of your portfolio.

Rick's Tip

Be careful if you're selling a security in your taxable account at a loss. This would trigger a wash sale if you buy the exact same security in your IRA, and the loss won't be allowed. In this situation, you want to buy another stock or stock fund but not the exact one you just sold at a loss.

In Shirley's case, we were able to move all of her bonds to her IRA account and replace the bonds with stock mutual funds in her taxable account. Using the asset allocation strategy advocated in the next section, we selected diversified stock mutual funds that complemented her other stock holdings. We also replaced the stock fund holdings she had that were underperforming or not already tax-efficient. By holding a small cash position and periodically selling portions of her stock funds to replenish it, she was able to take monthly distributions that equaled the income she'd been receiving.

Finally, we arranged to have her tax liability withheld from her RMD at the end of each year. This eliminated the need to make quarterly estimates. Paying the tax liability at the end of the year also allowed her to retain earnings on the tax payment longer than if she had to send in the money four times per year. Her cash flow improved significantly, and her total tax bill was reduced by 15%.

Rodgers' Recommendations for Transferring Highly Taxed Assets into Tax-Deferred Accounts

Decide on your allocation between stocks and bonds, then allocate all of your bonds to your tax-deferred accounts first.

Only use municipal bonds in your taxable account after you've filled your taxable accounts with bonds. If you're allocating part of your portfolio to real estate investment trusts, these securities should also be put into the taxable account.

When taking a withdrawal from your taxable account in a down market, simultaneously sell the same amount of bonds in the tax-deferred account as you do in the taxable account. Then use the proceeds to buy the security you've sold in the taxable account to maintain your overall stock position.

BEGIN TO BUILD YOUR INVESTMENT PLAN AROUND ASSET ALLOCATION

In 1986, Gary Brinson, Randolph Hood, and Gilbert Beebower analyzed 90 pension funds[2] and identified three primary investment strategies that determine variations in portfolio performance: (1) market timing, (2) security selection, and (3) asset allocation. Out of these three strategies, the two that have the *least* impact on performance variation are market timing and security selection, activities that rely on attempts to predict the future. Most stockbrokers' recommendations are based on these two strategies.

Wall Street firms spend billions of dollars each year trying to outguess their competition in these two areas. Yet on average, the

---

2   Gary P. Brinson, L. Randolph Hood, and Gilbert L. Beebower. "Determinants of Portfolio Performance," *Financial Analysts Journal* 42, no. 4 (July-August 1986): 39-44.

two strategies don't add value. In most studies, not only are they found to not add value, but especially after management fees are deducted, they significantly underperform the market.

The third strategy in the Brinson Hood Beebower study—asset allocation—has the largest effect on portfolio performance variation and is the simplest of the three to use. The Nobel-Prize winning economist Harry Markowitz used asset allocation as the basis of his *Modern Portfolio Theory* (MPT), which has become the standard for the best advisors in the business today; I'll describe both asset allocation and MPT in more detail in the next section.

The importance of asset allocation is evidenced in the annual study on Qualitative Analysis of Investor Behavior (QAIB) published by DALBAR, a firm that develops standards for—and provides research, ratings, and rankings of intangible factors to—the financial services industry. The QAIB effort began in 1994 to examine the returns investors actually realize and the behaviors that produce those returns. The 2005 QAIB study found an average retail mutual fund investor grew $10,000 to only $21,422 between 1987 and 2005, earning 3.9% per year. A buy and hold strategy using the S&P 500 index grew $10,000 into $94,555, in that same time, earning 11.9% per year.

The table below from the 2006 QAIB study[3] shows the one-year investor return for the 20-year period from 1987 to 2006.

Table 2.1 - One-year Investor Return, 1987-2006			
Year	Equity Investors	Fixed Income Investors	Asset Allocation Investors
1987	0.5	-0.8	6.0
1988	17.9	4.7	-1.8
1989	23.5	6.6	20.8
1990	-5.6	2.2	6.8
1991	29.4	11.9	17.3
1992	7.3	8.6	1.1
1993	15.9	7.9	16.7
1994	0.0	-5.0	-5.5
1995	26.5	14.4	25.4
1996	17.3	7.7	11.5
1997	20.6	8.1	16.0
1998	34.5	5.9	32.4
1999	26.6	-5.7	5.5
2000	-10.0	2.3	-2.9
2001	-14.8	-0.5	-6.2
2002	-21.9	2.7	-10.1
2003	29.8	4.2	17.7
2004	12.6	1.3	7.6
2005	8.3	-0.5	2.0
2006	14.7	2.0	10.9

These calculations assume investors start investing on January 1 of each year and withdraw their investment on December 31. The effect of compounding across years is therefore lost. Additionally, because of the year by year nature of the calculation, returns can't

3   DALBAR, Qualitative Analysis of Investor Behavior (QAIB) Report 2006, http://www.qaib.com (2006).

be asset weighted. This means the 0.5% return in 1987 is based on assets of $168 billion, while the 2006 return of 14.7% is based on assets of $5.9 trillion. The 2006 return clearly has far greater effect on wealth than the 1987 return.

Whether the mutual fund industry is enjoying rapid expansion in times of economic boom or is being battered by the bears, the key findings uncovered in DALBAR's first study remain true.

1. Investment return is far more dependent on investor behavior than on fund performance.

2. Mutual fund investors who hold their investments are more successful than those that time the market.

Asset allocation accounts for over 90% of the variation in returns of a diversified portfolio! So why isn't everyone using it? Many advisors continue to attempt to add value to your accounts through market-timing, otherwise known as active trading strategies; I'll go into more detail about active trading strategies in the next section. Advisors follow these traditional investment strategies, strategies all academic studies and publications—including this book—conclude don't work. Most stockbrokers and active managers simply don't understand the concepts featured in this book or choose to ignore them. Why?

Wall Street has become the accepted authority, and its wisdom goes unchallenged; the people who work on Wall Street have the mistaken impression that they are at the center of the financial universe. Huge salaries and extravagant livelihoods are based on the belief that active investment management adds value and is worth the cost. If Wall Street were to follow the concepts of investing utilizing asset classes, it would literally be out of business. Of course, nobody's going to rush to put the Street out of business, so an active strategy continues to be utilized. Yet active strategies engender investigation and analysis expenses and increase general transaction costs, including capital gains taxation. They also often require the acceptance of a relatively high degree of diversifiable risk.

Despite the overwhelming power of Wall Street, even the most senior members of the investment community have fortunately begun to question why asset allocation hasn't had more widespread acceptance.[4] It turns out the organizational politics of the major financial services firms have proven to be another formidable barrier to its acceptance.

Yet another barrier to asset allocation acceptance is the irrational behaviors many individual investors display. These behaviors make investors more likely to accept the advice of ill-informed financial planners. Be on the lookout for the following five irrational behaviors in yourself.

1. **Loss aversion.** If you expect to always find high returns with low risk, you're fooling yourself. Consider what happened in the summer of 1982, when large American banks lost close to all of their past earnings (cumulatively)—which amounted to just about everything ever made in the history of American banking. These banks had been lending to South and Central American countries that all defaulted at the same time—"an event of an exceptional nature."[5] It took just one summer to figure out that this was a sucker's business, and all of the earnings from these ventures came from a very risky game. The

---

4   Richard Michaud. "The Markowitz Optimization Enigma: Is 'Optimized' Optimal?," *Financial Analysts Journal* 45, no. 1 (January-February 1989): 31-42.

5   Richard Michaud. "The Markowitz Optimization Enigma: Is 'Optimized' Optimal?," *Financial Analysts Journal* 45, no. 1 (January-February 1989): 31-42.

bankers involved had led everyone, especially themselves, into believing they weren't taking high risks. They thought they were being conservative. In truth, they weren't conservative, just phenomenally skilled at self-deception. This travesty is repeating itself once again today, with the "risk-conscious" large banks again under financial strain after the real-estate subprime loan collapse.

2. **Narrow framing or tunneling.** This includes making decisions without considering all implications. *Avoid tunneling at all costs*, since it can take you off in a wrong direction. We're taught to focus like this is a principle for success, but focus too narrowly, and you miss the bigger picture.

3. **Anchoring.** This term means to relate to familiar experiences even when inappropriate, or to take undue risk in one area and avoid rational risk in others.

4. **Ineffective Diversification.** This is diversification in its worst sense: seeking to reduce risk, but by simply using different sources. It involves herding or copying the behavior of others, even in the face of unfavorable outcomes.

5. **Regret.** With regret, you treat errors of commission more seriously than errors of omission. You may have a tendency to react to news without reasonable examination.

6. **Optimism.** With optimism, you believe only good things happen to you, and bad things are meant for others.

Rodgers' Recommendations for Beginning to Build Your Investment Plan Around Asset Allocation

- Asset allocation is far more important than both market timing and security selection in making sure your portfolio performs well.

- Be aware that many advisors ignore asset allocation and instead engage in market timing—or active—trading strategies, because a flurry of activity makes it appear they're adding value to your account.

- Irrational behaviors on the part of investors themselves contribute to a reluctance to embrace asset allocation in favor of other ineffective strategies.

FIVE STEPS TO REDUCING THE WRONG KIND OF INVESTMENT RISK

A good way to avoid the irrational behaviors I described in the last section is to take the following five steps toward reducing your overall investment risk. Knowing and practicing these steps before potential problems arise can increase your odds of steering clear of actions that will hurt your retirement assets. Perhaps no one understands this better than Harry Markowitz.

Sixty years ago, Markowitz, a graduate student at the University of Chicago, developed the principle of Modern Portfolio Theory (MPT) based on his keen insight: risk (which he defined as volatility) must be the central focus for the whole process of investing. Markowitz observed an investment world blindly living in a paradox—while it was accepted that human beings, by nature, are risk-averse, investing had essentially ignored the interrelationship between risk and return. That is, to achieve returns, *risk is necessary*. But how can you control it?

MPT answers this question through its postulation that the total risk in a portfolio can be separated into two kinds of risk: uncompensated risk and compensated risk. Uncompensated risk (about 70% of total risk) is the possibility economic (and non-economic) news may uniquely impact the market price of a particular stock. For example, the price of Ford Motor Co. stock may go down as a result of the departure of a key Ford executive. Investors who hold only Ford stock can protect themselves against this risk by also owning stock in companies that are unaffected by the departure of Ford executives.

Compensated risk (about 30% of total risk) reflects the economic (and non-economic) news that impacts the market price of many or all stocks. Since the prices of individual stocks are affected, more or less, by the risk of a general rise or fall in the value of the stock market itself, compensated risk is unavoidable by an investor who invests in the stock market. When investors bear compensated risk, however, they expect to be rewarded for doing so.

Markowitz was subsequently awarded the Nobel Prize for Economic Sciences in 1990. Merton H. Miller, who shared the prize, called their theory the "Big Bang of modern finance." Indeed, investment managers began to apply techniques of the theory in the late 1960s, and by the 1970s, they had become commonplace. Now taught in virtually every graduate business school in the country, Modern Portfolio Theory stipulates if you're going to take the risks of the stock market, you need to be compensated for those risks.

In terms of your own retirement assets, the question you should be asking is, *how can I protect my portfolio from uncompensated risk while in pursuit of higher returns?* Most advisors have no idea they can eliminate virtually all uncompensated risk and reduce overall volatility by following an investment process that utilizes the following five steps.

Asset Class Investing

An asset class is simply a group of securities that share common risk and return characteristics. Asset class investing involves the construction of portfolios that reliably deliver the returns of a specific asset class. This is done by investing in all, or most of, the securities within the asset category under consideration. There's no subjective forecasting of the stock market or economic conditions, and no attempt to distinguish between "undervalued" and "overvalued" securities. Securities are considered for purchase when they meet the asset class parameters defined by the investment manager, and they're considered for sale when they don't.

The three main asset classes include: cash/money markets; bonds; and stocks. While these asset classes appear in an order that's generally the safest to the most risky, remember there's no absolute ranking of risk in the equity market. Let's take a closer look at each of the classes now.

Cash/Money Market

The first asset class, *cash*, includes money market funds, which are made up of T-Bills, certificates of deposit (CDs), and commercial paper. These investments are called cash because the net asset value (NAV) is always one dollar; in other words, the price doesn't fluctuate. Few people understand when their holdings are in cash, they're also invested in an asset class—the U.S. dollar.

Bonds

Also called fixed-income, this asset class is divided into two main groups: stable bonds such as U.S. Government and AAA corporate bonds; certificates of deposits (CDs); tax-free municipal bonds; and higher yield bonds such as corporate bonds and junk bonds. For my clients, I generally recommend only the first group. Within this category, my client and I decide if we want long-term, intermediate, or shorter duration bonds. I recommend short-term bonds, meaning five to seven years or less to maturity, because a short duration fund will give you 94% of the return without the long-term bond volatility. If you're in a long-term bond fund and interest rates move up, your fund can drop 25% in a day.

I also prefer my clients own the individual bonds themselves rather than through a fund. Owning the individual bond gives you a fixed interest rate and a fixed date in the future when you know you'll get your principal returned in full.

Rick's Tip

Never invest in junk bonds; it's not worth the risk. All you'll be doing is adding volatility without gaining the expected returns of a stock. I never recommend junk bonds because they're actually unsecured loans of a company. In the case of a company that goes bankrupt, that company's secured bond-holders will be paid before stockholders, but this won't be the case with junk bond owners.

Stocks

After cash and bonds, we subdivide asset classes into more specific categories distinguished by their unique characteristics. Equity, or stock, asset classes are often categorized according to the size of their market capitalization (number of outstanding shares multiplied by current stock price). What stocks go into an asset class? The way the academics built equity asset classes is quite involved. First, they took all of the companies on the New York Stock Exchange, ranked them by size, and then divided them into ten deciles. They designated the largest one tenth of the companies as Decile Number 1, including companies on the scale of General Electric or Chrysler. Decile Number 2 represented the next 10% graduating down in company size. Deciles 9 and 10 were the smallest companies, the bottom 20% in size. That's not an asset class yet, but it's part of an asset class.

Next, they looked at the NASDAQ and the American stock exchange, and they filled in the same capitalization requirements that were in Deciles 1 through 10. Deciles 1 through 5 qualify as large company stocks; small company stocks are in the 6 through 10 deciles. Deciles 9 and 10 on the NASDAQ and American stock exchange have over 2,000 small stocks. The academic asset class of value stocks originally included every value stock, across all those same markets. They discovered that was too cumbersome, so they divided it into asset classes called "large value" and "small value." The same applies to "growth" and "international" equity asset classes. Asset classes for stocks are further refined in this way according to their potential total return over time. Some of the primary asset classes include:

- **Large-Cap Growth.** These are very large companies that are doing very well (they have an average capitalization of approximately $7 billion or greater). This type of company usually has good sales, good prospects for the future, and good earnings.

- **U.S. Large-Cap Value.** These are large U.S. publicly traded companies that may be temporarily out of favor. They aren't doing well by any measure and are distressed economically.

- **U.S. Small-Cap Growth.** These are U.S. publicly traded smaller companies with an average capitalization of less than $2 billion. They have good sales and good prospects for the future.

- **U.S. Small-Cap Value.** These are U.S. publicly traded smaller companies (with an average capitalization of less than $2 billion) that aren't doing very well.

- **Standard & Poor's (S & P) 500.** There's generally a lot of confusion between asset classes and indexes, but there *is* a distinction. Asset classes are academically defined, whereas an index is simply a numerical group of stocks. Indexes are commercial benchmarks. The S&P 500 is an index of 500 stocks. We also call it an equity asset class, even though it contains both large growth and large value stocks. It's well known and gives people something to compare to.

- **International.** The last two equity asset classes are international large and small. This group generally comprises stocks of companies based outside the U.S.—from any part of the world with established free markets.

- **International Large.** International large companies that are doing very well, including growth to value stocks and everything in between.

- **International Small.** International small companies also include both growth and value stocks that aren't doing so well.

Asset class funds are called passively managed, which means there's no "active" decision-making occurring about buying and selling the issues that are contained within the mutual fund. Their sole purpose is to mimic the markets while experiencing very low turnover.

On the flip side, actively managed mutual funds (especially the advertised ones that appeal to the retail market) tend to do what we call *style drift*. Active managers are under tremendous pressure to deliver returns, even though that may not be the function of a particular fund. They'll drift out of their asset class into another asset class in an effort to hopefully boost their returns.

It's very difficult to maintain a balanced portfolio with actively managed funds because of style drift. Let's say you wanted a portfolio that's a 50-50 mix of large-growth companies and small-value companies. If the manager of the fund of large-growth companies starts buying small-value companies because large growth isn't doing well, or vice versa, that skews your 50-50 allocation.

In addition, if every fund went to large growth when growth is doing well, then growth plummets, your whole portfolio would plummet. That's why many investors lost 40-70% when the technology bubble burst in the 2000-2002 market. They may have tried to remain diversified, but the managers of those funds drifted. If each one fudged just a little in the direction of whatever was up at the time, it would be enough to cause big trouble in a portfolio.

Another example is how most 401(k) plans are sold. Normally, the provider offers a list of mutual funds from which participants may choose. This is to avoid any liability if something goes wrong. Participants, without any knowledge or advice, naturally pick the funds with the best returns for the last period, and that's how they end up with everything in one asset class.

The best way to do asset class investing is by owning asset class mutual funds or institutional asset class mutual funds, because they're more reliable in concentrating on a specific asset class. These funds are a relatively new hybrid, created by institutional money managers. Although not available to the general public, institutional asset class mutual funds can be purchased by participants through selected groups of investment advisors who are required to educate their clients on the benefits of passive asset class investing.

There are three major attributes of institutional asset class funds that attract institutional investors.

- **Lower operating expenses.** All mutual funds and separately managed accounts have expenses that include management fees, administrative charges, and custody fees. These are expressed as a percentage of assets. According to Morningstar, the average annual expense ratio for all retail equity mutual funds is 1.54%. In comparison, the same ratio for institutional asset class funds is typically only about one-third of all retail equity mutual funds. All other factors being equal, lower costs lead to higher rates of return.

- **Lower turnover resulting in lower cost.** Most investment managers do a lot of active trading, thinking this adds value. The average retail mutual fund has a turnover ratio of 83%. This means, on average, 83% of the securities in the portfolio are traded over a 12-month period. This represents $83,000 of traded securities for every $100,000 invested. Higher turnover is costly to shareholders, because each time a trade is made, there are transaction costs, including commissions, spreads, and market impact costs. These hidden costs may amount to more than a fund's total operating expenses if the fund trades heavily, or if it invests in small company stocks for which trading costs are very high. Institutional asset class funds have significantly lower turnover, because their institutional investors want them to deliver a specific asset class return with as low a cost as possible.

- **Lower turnover resulting in lower taxes.** If a mutual fund sells a security for a gain, it must make a capital gains distribution to shareholders, because mutual funds are required to distribute 98% of their taxable income each year, including realized gains, to stay tax-exempt at the corporate level. They distribute all of their income annually, because no mutual fund manager wants to have his or her performance reduced by paying corporate income taxes.

Asset Allocation

Asset allocation simply means determining what proportion of your money is going to be invested in which asset classes—stocks, bonds, and cash investments—in order to maximize the growth of your portfolio for each unit of risk you take. As I mentioned earlier, this may be the single most important determinant of the long-term performance of any investment portfolio.

Rick's Tip

The Brinson et al. study I referenced on page 44 also revealed when two portfolios have the same arithmetic average return, the portfolio with smaller up and down swings in value (less volatility) will have a greater compound return. Moreover, it showed 94% of performance was attributable to the allocation of the assets. The study's authors found even choosing the right individual asset added less than 6% to the returns. The factor that made the greatest difference was the combination or allocation of asset classes.

Some critics of asset allocation see this balance as settling for mediocrity, but for most investors, it's the best protection against major loss should things ever go amiss in one investment class or sub-class. The consensus among most informed financial professionals is that asset allocation is one of the most important decisions investors make.

Allocating your assets is simple. The first step is to identify what asset classes are represented by the mutual funds. Then you can spread, or allocate, your money among them to minimize risk. How do you determine what percentage of each asset class you should own? For every level of risk, there's some optimum combination of investments that will give you the highest rate of return. The combinations of investments exhibiting this optimal risk/ reward trade-off form what we call the *efficient frontier.*

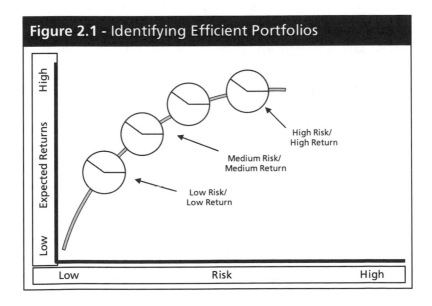

Figure 2.1 - Identifying Efficient Portfolios

You can choose how much volatility you're willing to bear in your portfolio by picking any other point that falls on the efficient frontier. This will give you the maximum return for the amount of risk you wish to accept. Optimizing your portfolio isn't something you can calculate in your head. There are computer programs that are dedicated to determining optimal portfolios by estimating hundreds (and sometimes thousands) of different expected returns for each given amount of risk. Your financial advisor should be able to offer you an effective program for determining your own optimal portfolio.

Diversification

The most common definition for diversification is not putting all of your eggs (i.e., your investments) in one basket. A truly diversified portfolio is comprised of many asset classes, some of which are doing well, and some of which aren't.

Some investors believe they've effectively diversified simply by holding a number of different stocks. They don't realize they're in for an emotional roller-coaster ride if these investments share similar risk factors by belonging to the same industry group or asset class. For instance, "diversification" among many high-tech companies isn't diversification at all.

Rick's Tip

Although concentrated ownership of founders' stock sometimes conveys fabulous riches to a fortunate few—e.g., Microsoft's Bill Gates—it's impossible to know ahead of time which firms will grow from unseasoned start-ups to Fortune 500 companies. In fact, it's reasonable to expect a great percentage of new companies will fail.

I've found most investors are surprised to learn asset classes switch places, variably outperforming each other. In general, I see most people load up on blue chip stocks, which fall under the large cap growth asset class I mentioned earlier (which, by the way, is the most common type of asset sold to them by their stockbrokers). Why is this? Because large cap stocks are the names that are the most recognizable, like GM, Wal-Mart, Microsoft, and General Electric.

If all of your money is in several investments, yet in only one asset class, then your investment portfolio is *ineffectively* diversified, meaning all of your funds move together, and you really only have one asset class investment. Only when each of your investments move independently in the market can your portfolio be *effectively* diversified; see Step 4 below for a more detailed discussion on this. A diversified portfolio provides stability and, hence, a larger long-term return, but only if you spread your money among the various asset classes that don't always have the same price movements—for example, between value and growth; small and large; or international growth and value. Therefore, the total return of a diversified portfolio will never be as good as the current best asset class, nor will it ever be as poor as the worst. But the overall ride will be smoother, and the end result will be a superior return.

Effective Diversification

Almost all diversification is good, but the academics have refined it down to what they call *effective* and *ineffective* diversification. Again, an example of ineffective diversification is the investor who holds Microsoft stock and decides to diversify by investing in Dell and six other similar computer companies. If anything affects the computer industry, all the investments will be *positively correlated* to move together, either up or down.

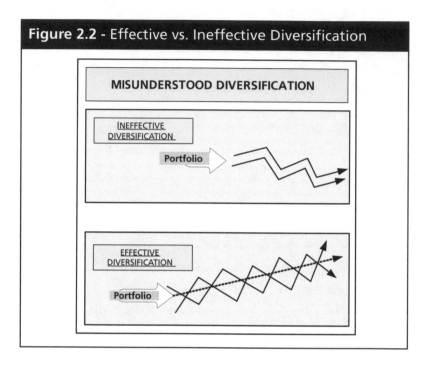

Figure 2.2 - Effective vs. Ineffective Diversification

MISUNDERSTOOD DIVERSIFICATION

INEFFECTIVE DIVERSIFICATION

Portfolio

EFFECTIVE DIVERSIFICATION

Portfolio

Effective diversification means selecting asset classes with a low correlation to each other—an approach Harry Markowitz acknowledged when he stated that while almost all diversification is good, there's effective diversification and ineffective diversification.

The line charts above show the increases and decreases of value for two portfolios over time. The top chart shows ineffective diversification, in which the portfolios change in tandem with each other, and the second chart demonstrates effective diversification, in which the two portfolios move opposite to each other.

Overall, the charts indicate that two equal investments can have the same arithmetic rate of return but have very different ending values because of volatility. If your investments move up and down together, they are ineffectively diversified, which has the same effect as if they were all invested in just one fund. Chances are, there's tremendous stock overlap in these two ineffectively diversified funds as well.

Selecting asset classes with a low correlation to each other—i.e., effective diversification—is the Nobel Prize-winning secret for achieving more consistent portfolio performance. Again, academics have actually calculated methods to measure correlation in a portfolio, thereby enabling the volatility or risk of a portfolio to be measured with greater degrees of predictability. You want to design your portfolio so it has as little volatility as necessary to achieve your goals.

Rebalancing

Most investors and their advisors hold fast to the belief that they should keep their winners and sell their losers. This leads to portfolios with a large majority of current winners that become losers when the market turns, which it always does.

Rebalancing is a disciplined process of selling the winning asset classes and repositioning the proceeds into the so-called "losing" asset classes—an automatic version of selling high and buying low, which is how you ultimately win at investing.

The principle of rebalancing is to maintain the same percentages in the various asset classes you've chosen, to maintain proper diversification in all market environments. By rebalancing, you may give up some short-term gains if you reduce your holdings of winning stocks prematurely, but you'll also miss the big losses if and when they collapse.

The way to rebalance your original portfolio is to review it regularly with your advisor. You want to rebalance when the stock markets are reaching new highs, so you can harvest the gains in your stocks. This is the time to move some of those gains to the bond side of your portfolio, so you don't give all of your gains back the next time the stock market sells off. You also want to do this in the most tax-effective manner through harvesting losses in the taxable accounts and placing the bonds in your tax-deferred accounts.

Before the tech bubble burst, many smart investment advisors rebalanced their equity positions down to their allocation targets as the bull market pushed equity values upward. They increased equity positions as the declining markets dropped those positions below targets. As a result, they were selling high, then buying low. See the logic? When the price is down, you're able to buy more shares. Plus, you're reinvesting the money you've made along with your principal and compounding your growth.

Ricks' Tip

Studies show more frequent rebalancing improves results, which would indicate that a style that's outperforming the broad market doesn't stay in favor for long periods of time. The same holds true for a style that's underperforming the broad market: its out-of-favor status doesn't sustain for long periods of time.

Rebalancing an investment portfolio seems simple on the surface, but as you start to think through the method, frequency, tolerance limits, fees, and commissions, the subject reveals itself to be quite complex and without easy answers. Your advisor should be knowledgeable about the various issues surrounding rebalancing, and, ideally, should be able to explain them to you in a way that makes the desired method acceptable and practical to apply.

Rodgers' Recommendations for Reducing the Wrong Kind of Investment Risk

These five steps work together to level out the up-and-down ride associated with good and bad markets, producing steadier overall results.

1. Asset Class Investing
2. Asset Allocation
3. Diversification
4. Effective Diversification
5. Rebalancing

These powerful investment strategies work equally well for conservative, moderate, or aggressive investors. You can use them to build your own portfolio for retirement, to protect your assets once you've retired, or to meet other financial goals. Amazingly, the strategies actually simplify the investment decision-making process.

HOW TO INVEST IN A TAX-EFFICIENT WAY

Now let's discuss how to ensure your investment portfolio is efficient not just from a risk perspective, but from a tax standpoint as well. You may not be able to control the market, but you do have a lot of control over your taxes. By understanding basic tax rules and using tax-efficient investment strategies, you can minimize the annual tax bite on your taxable accounts.

The most tax-efficient investment strategy is simple: hold shares for as long as possible, thus deferring the taxes on your capital gains until you sell. An extremely tax-efficient portfolio would therefore be a selection of growth stocks you bought and held for the long haul. In this case, growth stocks would be preferred, because they tend to pay little or no dividends. Your return would be mostly made up of long-term capital gains. Best of all, you'd get to decide when you pay the tax by choosing when to sell them.

However, a portfolio full of growth stocks isn't without problems. For starters, concentration in few securities and the lack of diversification from being in mostly one asset class create volatility. You need the diversification of a balanced portfolio over several asset classes to reduce this volatility. It's important to keep in mind, then, that investing tax-efficiently is a balancing act. Though the reality is there will always be trade-offs, your overarching goal should be to minimize taxes while still attempting to achieve superior investment returns.

Another issue with long-term investments is they tend to scare some investors into holding even when it's not wise to do so, since these investors believe selling would trigger additional capital gains. Remember, *the tax decision should never overrule the investment decision.* Assessing the tax consequences of your investments at each stage—contribution, accumulation, and distribution—is the key to success in the world of tax-advantaged investing. Just don't lose sight of the investment return like one of my clients, Joe Mitchell, unfortunately did.

Case Study: Joe Mitchell, investor

Joe Mitchell had accumulated a large position in Dell Inc., the computer company. He purchased most of the stock in the 1990s, and through several stock splits, he'd accumulated over $250,000 worth of the stock with a total cost of $50,000.

The stock had been doing well until 2005, when the stock price started heading south. By the middle of the year, Joe's Dell stock was down over 10%, yet the stock market was still going up. Still, Joe refused to sell any of the stock, because he didn't want to pay capital gains tax. By the end of the year, his stock value had fallen to less than $178,000, and the stock market was up that year by 4.9%.

Had Joe sold the stock when it was down 10%, he would have owed $26,000 in capital gains tax ($225,000 - $50,000 = $175,000 X 15%). He would have been left with $199,000 that could have gained back 4.9% in an index fund.

Joe's mistake is easy to see in hindsight (the perfect vision!). Of course, you won't know at the time if the stock's going to recover or if the investment you choose with the proceeds is going to perform better than the one you just sold. But in Joe's case, the stock was moving at such a sharp contrast to the stock market's overall direction, he should have at least sold part of the position by mid-year. Dell went on to lose 16% in 2006 (S&P 500 +15.8%) and another 2% in 2007 (S&P 500 +5.5%). Again, investment reasons should always trump tax reasons.

Rick's Tip

If mutual funds are the building blocks of a portfolio, tax-efficient investing begins with the simple notion that good fund managers who are sensitive to tax issues can make a difference on your after-tax return. A "good manager," from a tax perspective, harvests losses, pays attention to the holding period, and controls the fund's turnover rate. Studies show the average actively managed mutual fund operates at 85% tax efficiency.

Most fund managers are tasked solely with generating a return. They don't think about working with taxable and non-taxable portfolios, and they don't care about short-term gains. Of course, in your IRA or 401(k), you don't care about short-

term gains either, but short-term gains in a taxable account can be disastrous. However, mutual fund managers are often not as concerned as you are with keeping taxes low. These professionals are concentrating on maximizing pre-tax—not after-tax—returns. The difference is an important one.

It's clear the best after-tax returns start with the best pre-tax returns, but even the fund industry itself has come around to the need for examining after-tax returns. Let's dig in with an explanation of the more tax-efficient types of funds.

Index Funds

Index mutual funds are designed to match the performance and risk characteristics of a market benchmark like the Standard & Poor's (S&P) 500 Index. They've long been the easiest way to construct a tax-smart portfolio. Index funds don't need to do much buying and selling, because the makeup of the portfolio changes only when the underlying benchmark changes. Since the portfolio turnover in these funds is low, stock index funds can often reduce an investor's tax exposure. But investors should understand there are few absolutes: index funds can also realize gains. When a security is removed from a fund's target index, stock in the company must be sold by the fund and new stock purchased. Index funds also tend to have lower expense ratios because they aren't actively managed. Lower expenses mean you get to keep more of the gain in your pocket.

Exchange Traded Funds

Exchange traded funds (ETFs) are a popular alternative to mutual funds due to their tax efficiency and lower operating fees. The fact ETFs offer more control over management of gains is very attractive to the tax-efficient investor. ETFs look like index funds but trade like stocks. The most popular ETFs use broad market benchmarks such as the S&P 500 Index or the Nasdaq 100 (QQQQs or Qubes). There are ETFs that represent nearly all parts of the market (midsized value, small growth, and foreign companies) as well as various sectors (telecom, utilities, technology).

Most ETFs have even lower expenses than their index fund counterparts. Unlike mutual funds, ETFs can be bought and sold throughout the day, rather than just at the end of trading. ETFs tend to have little turnover, few capital gains distributions, and a low dividend yield—making them very tax-efficient.

In addition, ETFs are not vulnerable to the hysteria of other investors because liquidity is provided through the stock market. When the stock market declines, many investors panic and pull out. Mutual fund managers are then forced to sell positions to provide cash to the sellers. Those shareholders that keep their shares suffer a double whammy—a loss of market value, and taxable gains created by the manager selling securities in the fund. Many investors have no idea this can happen. Yet ETFs don't have to sell securities to meet redemptions.

Despite their benefits, ETFs pose a problem for individual investors in the sense that ETFs aren't no-load. Rather, you have to pay commissions to buy and sell them. If you're investing regular sums over time, those costs can easily negate any break you get on annual expenses. ETFs are a better bet for those with a lump sum to invest.

Tax-efficient Mutual Funds

Some types of mutual funds are more tax-friendly than others. Tax-efficient mutual funds, for example, are managed by professional fund managers who attempt to minimize the buying and selling of securities and thus are less likely to pass along taxable gains to individual investors. These professionals use a variety of strategies and objectives, including indexing and careful security selection, to offset most capital gains with capital losses.

These funds are actively managed, but by good managers who pay attention to the tax ramifications of their trading. Some simply keep turnover low, minimizing the capital gains they have to realize. Others try to match the sale of any winners with dumping their losers, so gains can be offset by losses.

Rick's Tip

You can still rebalance in a taxable account. As long as you've held the stocks or stock funds at least a year, you'll benefit from a lower capital gains rate. This allows you to improve your investment portfolio without major suffering at tax time. Many investors unknowingly expose themselves to unnecessarily high rates of income taxes when they sell shares from their taxable investment account at a profit and haven't held the position for 12 months. One strategy for rebalancing in taxable accounts is to take all distributions in cash instead of reinvesting the distributions back into the original fund. The cash can be used to invest in the underweighted parts of the portfolio. This avoids the need to sell positions to rebalance.

Review Your Portfolio

Tax-efficient investing requires active involvement. That starts with looking for tax-efficient mutual funds as discussed above. You also need to monitor the portfolios so losses are harvested to offset gains. In addition, you must pay attention to holding periods to ensure the asset has been held at least 12 months.

Start by screening your funds for performance and then for tax efficiency. Separate your list of funds that meet your performance criteria by tax efficiency. You don't want to completely exclude funds that aren't tax-efficient, because these can be held in your tax-deferred accounts. You don't need or want to be in a tax-efficient fund with your qualified retirement plan. Remember the trade offs I mentioned earlier between performance and tax efficiency? Returns tend to be lower in tax-efficient funds. Inside a qualified plan, you want the managers to be more aggressive and make moves in the portfolio that, if they considered the tax consequences, they might choose not to make.

One of the biggest mistakes investors make is failing to harvest losses in their portfolio. A lot of people think just because an investment is worth less than they paid for it, they haven't really lost any money, because they didn't sell it. Tell that to the holders of Enron stock! You should start by evaluating the investment. If you had cash today, would you still invest in that same position, or are there other opportunities that look better? If the answer is no, take the loss and reinvest elsewhere. The loss could be worth thousands in saved taxes. The reason most investors don't use this strategy is because loss harvesting is labor intensive—and nobody wants to admit to taking a loss.

Rodgers' Recommendations for Investing in a Tax-Efficient Way

- Investing tax-efficiently is a balancing act between diversified asset classes that minimize taxes yet still achieve superior returns.
- The tax decision should never overrule the investment decision.
- Index funds, exchange traded funds, and tax-efficient mutual funds are all good tax-efficient investment choices.

- In terms of your retirement accounts, tax efficiency shouldn't be your goal; your retirement account investments should be more aggressive so they result in bigger returns over the long haul.

- Review your portfolio regularly, and don't be afraid to harvest losses—especially since you may be able to take the losses as a tax write-off.

IMPLEMENT A ZERO TAX BRACKET APPROACH

Fortunately, President George W. Bush's tax legislation made it much easier to construct a tax-efficient portfolio. The initial act came in 2003 with the Jobs and Growth Tax Relief Reconciliation Act (JGTRRA) of 2003, which was then extended by the Tax Increase Prevention and Reconciliation Act (TIPRA) of 2005. These tax cuts drove the top federal capital gains rate down to 15% and made the same rate apply to dividends issued by domestic stocks and mutual funds. And if your taxable income puts you in the 10%-15% bracket (that's $67,900 for married filing jointly in 2009, half that for singles), your capital gains and dividends rate is zero in 2009 and 2010. (Keep in mind payouts from foreign stocks and real estate investment trusts don't qualify for the dividend tax break; for maximum tax efficiency, these investments should be held in tax-advantaged retirement accounts.) You can read about these breaks in the following case study about my clients Bob and Carolyn Whitehall.

Case Study: Bob and Carolyn Whitehall, retirees

When Bob Whitehall retired from a regional bank in 1997, he'd accumulated a comfortable nest egg of $1.8 million dollars. A third of his savings was in the common stock of his employer; the bank offered an employee stock purchase program that allowed him to invest in the stock through payroll deduction. The stock had done well over the years, paying cash and stock dividends, which Bob reinvested while he was working. After retirement, Bob began to take the dividends in cash and used them to supplement his income.

In early 2008, Bob and Carolyn reached their mid-70s, and they came to me for an evaluation of their investment portfolio. I found it was still worth $1.8 million. One third of it was invested in three rental properties; another third was still in the bank's 401(k) plan Bob never rolled over; and the remaining third was invested in various stocks, mutual funds, and bank certificates of deposit (CDs). Bob also still had $500,000 invested in the bank stock that was divided between the 401(k) and the taxable accounts.

Despite only taking modest distributions over the years, the portfolio hadn't appreciated at all. The bank stock had done poorly since his retirement, but Bob refused to sell it because he hated paying capital gains tax. The stock had a very low cost basis because he'd accumulated it over many years, and stock dividends aren't taxable until the shares are sold. Still, Bob thought he was being savvy by keeping the stock and not paying capital gains tax.

The reality is the purchasing power of his nest egg had shrunk to $1.3 million because of inflation. Allowing this to continue would eventually reduce Bob and Carolyn's standard of living. If one or both of them ended up in a nursing home, they could see the entire nest egg wiped out in ten years.

Fortunately, there was an answer that helped even someone like Bob who hated to pay capital gains tax. Today, ordinary income tax rates for individuals ranged from 10% to 35%. As I mentioned above, certain capital gains and qualified dividends (i.e., adjusted net capital gains) are taxed at 15% for taxpayers in the 25% bracket or higher and 5% for taxpayers in the 15% or 10% tax brackets.

Pursuant to JGTRRA and extended by TIPRA, the 5% rate drops to 0% from 2008 through 2010. In 2011, all of these rates revert back to the levels prior to 2001 unless Congress acts to extend the law, which is highly uncertain. This allows us a three-year window to take advantage of the 0% rate.

In 2009, the 0% rate applies to taxable income up to $33,950 for single taxpayers. The threshold is $67,900 for married couples filing jointly. This number refers to the net taxable income after itemized deductions, as opposed to adjusted gross income (AGI). Thus, a joint filer with an AGI of $100,000 may still be able to take advantage of the 0% bracket if they have itemized deductions of $32,100. That level of deductions isn't difficult to get to if you live in a state that has a high income tax, hold a mortgage on your home, or are charitably minded.

Additionally, you can exceed the taxable income and still receive a partial benefit from the 0% bracket because the portion of your capital gain that's below the threshold would still qualify for the 0% rate. For example, a joint filer with $40,000 in long-term capital gains and $40,000 in other income after deductions would have $27,900 of the gain taxed at 0% and $12,100 taxed at 15%.

My strategy for Bob and Carolyn was to reposition the portfolio to place most of their income-producing assets into their tax-deferred accounts. This significantly reduced their taxable ordinary income, which allowed us to sell more of the stock at the 0% capital gains rate. We sold the bank stock in the 401(k) that had no tax implications and used the proceeds to buy CDs and other fixed income assets, so they could maintain a balanced investment strategy when investing in tax-efficient investments in the taxable accounts.

Bob wanted to keep some of the bank stock for sentimental reasons, so we agreed to keep $100,000 in the stock. The balance of the stock in their taxable account will be sold in thirds in 2008-2010. Bob will still have to pay capital gains tax on some of the sales proceeds, but he's learning to appreciate the wisdom of evaluating performance on an after-tax basis! It'll be harder for taxpayers who are still working to take advantage of the 0% tax bracket because of the limitations in manipulating earned income.

Retirees who are living on investment income have the most opportunities. Yet one of the challenges for retirees drawing Social Security benefits is structuring income that doesn't make their benefits taxable. This is one of the problems with tax-free municipal bond income—income from municipal bonds is used in the calculation to determine the taxability of Social Security benefits. When calculating the 0% rate on capital gains, municipal income doesn't count.

Rick's Tip

Retirees drawing Social Security benefits need to take care in determining the amount of capital gains they can realize and stay in the 0% bracket. Capital gains is income that is used to determine how much of your Social Security is taxed. You can review the upcoming section on Understanding Social Security to familiarize yourself with the calculation used to tax benefits.

Realizing an additional $10,000 in capital gains could make $5,000 more of your Social Security subject to tax and potentially put you over the 0% bracket. Retirees who are already in a low tax bracket should consider investing in dividend-paying stocks instead, because they can provide much needed inflation-fighting growth potential, as well as untaxed income.

Gifting Appreciated Securities

You can make the most of the 0% bracket by searching for positions that have the least amount of capital gains. This will allow you to raise the highest amount of tax-free cash. It's an especially desirable method for those retirees who have a significant amount of their assets tied up in tax-deferred accounts.

Higher tax bracket investors may want to consider gifting appreciated securities to other family members in the lower tax bracket. If you're considering this strategy, keep in mind the maximum amount you can gift to any one individual without filing a gift tax return is $13,000 in 2009. A husband and wife could gift a total $26,000 to each child. This amount is adjusted for inflation each year, but only in $1,000 increments.

New kiddie-tax rules also went into effect in 2008, and they're much more restrictive than before. Full-time students under age 24 will be subject to tax at the parents' rates with few exceptions. One of those exceptions is if the child earns income and contributes more than 50% of the cost of his or her support. In this situation, a parent should gift appreciated securities to the student to be sold to pay for college rather than help the student pay for tuition out of pocket. The parent would then be paying for tuition with tax-free dollars using the student's 0% bracket on the capital gain.

Parents who have been helping their adult children fund Roth IRAs should also consider gifting appreciated securities to the child if the child is in the lower tax brackets. The child could then sell the gifted securities to fund the Roth IRA. The ultimate cost to the parent of funding the Roth IRA is less, because again, the parent is taking advantage of the child's 0% rate on the capital gain.

This same strategy applies to higher income taxpayers who are helping to support their elderly parents that have low taxable income. The taxpayers can transfer appreciated securities to Mom and Dad, who can, in turn, sell the securities to pay for living expenses.

Higher income individuals may want to consider gifting securities with the most amount of appreciation to charities to lower their taxable income. If you aren't comfortable with giving the securities outright to a charity, consider setting up a Charitable Remainder Unit Trust (CRUT). Gifting securities to a CRUT is a completed gift and will qualify for a partial tax deduction. A CRUT allows the donor to receive an income stream for life from the gift. The asset is released from the CRUT when the donor passes away. The amount of the deduction is based on the size of the income stream retained by the donor and the donor's life expectancy. Income received from the CRUT is only partially taxable, because part of it is considered a return of capital.

Rick's Tip

Keep in mind although the 0% tax rate is scheduled to last through 2010, conditions could change. For this reason, you should begin implementing your 0% bracket strategies as soon as possible. You don't want to delay the strategies until 2010, only to find out the law changed before then. Congress is always looking for money, and there's a chance tax rates could go much higher on capital gains.

Rodgers' Recommendations for a Zero Tax Bracket Approach

- Taxpayers in the lower income brackets should plan now to take advantage of the 0% rate on long-term capital gains and qualified dividends.

- Higher income taxpayers should look for gifting opportunities to pass appreciated assets to other family members in the lower tax bracket or charities.

- Beware of the tax on Social Security benefits when planning your capital gains strategy. More of your benefits may become taxable and negate a portion of the 0% rate.

- Tax laws may change sooner than the current 2010 deadline. You don't want to miss the opportunity to pay no tax on long-term capital gains.

* * *

You now have two of the three legs of the stool under your belt (great work!), but in order to make the stool truly sturdy, you need to know about the all-important Leg Three—tax-free savings—which I cover in-depth in the next section.

Chapter 3

Leg Three: Tax-Free Savings Strategies

UNDERSTANDING ROTH ACCOUNTS

Tax-Free Savings Strategies is the final leg of my Three-Legged Stool™ Approach. The main components of this leg are Roth IRAs and Roth 401(k)s. Young or old, you should be constantly looking for ways to use the Roth to control you tax burden both now and in the future. These accounts are the premier individual retirement planning tools and savings accounts offered today, for several reasons I discuss below.

Roth IRAs

Unlike traditional IRAs or 401(k)s, withdrawals from Roth IRAs after age 59½ are generally not taxed, since you make your contributions to a Roth with after-tax dollars. The Roth IRA has flexible withdrawal rules that allow you to take out contributions (but not earnings) for any reason without penalty or taxes. Once you reach age 59½ and have had the account open for five years, you can withdraw your earnings tax- and penalty-free.

The problem with the Roth IRA is meeting the eligibility rules to contribute money to it. These rules require you to have earned income—but not too much. In 2009, eligibility phases out for a joint filer with modified adjusted gross income, or MAGI, between $166,000 and $176,000. For a single filer, the phase out is between MAGI of $105,000 and $120,000. The contribution limits and phase out levels are indexed to inflation after 2009, although the contribution levels will only increase in $1,000 increments. Like traditional IRAs, the Roth IRA allows 2009 contributions of $5,000 per person for those who qualify ($6,000 if you're age 50 or older at the end of the year).

Rick's Tip

Taxpayers with MAGIs under $100,000 (joint or single) can convert assets from their traditional IRA accounts into a Roth. I will cover these conversions in more detail in the next section.

Unlike traditional IRAs, there are no age limits for making contributions to a Roth IRA. A taxpayer who still has earned income isn't allowed to make contributions to a traditional IRA once he reaches age 70½. However, the taxpayer can continue to make contributions to a Roth IRA (as long as he doesn't exceed the income limits mentioned above). There are also no minimum distribution requirements at age 70½ for a Roth IRA. You can allow the money to continue to grow tax-free as long as you want.

An IRA account (traditional or Roth) is more flexible than a 401(k) and many other retirement plans. You can invest it in almost whatever you want, from stocks and mutual funds to bonds and real estate. This is a huge advantage when you're attempting to construct an efficient investment strategy.

Roth 401(k)s

Many employers are now offering Roth 401(k)s to their employees. As with Roth IRAs, there's no up-front tax deduction, but withdrawals are tax-free in retirement if you meet the same rules as listed above. The big advantage of the Roth 401(k) is there are no income-eligibility limits and you can potentially make larger contributions. Like traditional 401(k)s, employees can contribute up to $16,500 in 2009, plus an extra $5,500 if they're 50 or older.

Roth Accounts for Younger People

The smartest move a younger person can make is to invest in a Roth IRA. A person who starts saving $5,000 per year in a Roth IRA at age 20 will have over $1.5 million at age 60 if it grows at 8%. Provided the person has followed the rules, he won't owe the IRS a nickel on any of the money.

Many taxpayers, young and old, find it difficult to give up the immediate tax savings they'd receive if they chose to make a traditional IRA contribution that's deductible. In the example above, if the same person contributed to a traditional IRA, the entire $1.5 million would be taxable. He'd have saved about $50,000 in taxes along the way but would owe over $200,000 in taxes when he tried to spend any of the money.

As the example demonstrates, there's no doubt the Roth IRA is a better choice for a younger person. In addition, a Roth contribution is a great way to gift money to your children or grandchildren as long as they have earned income. In addition to the long-term, tax-free growth your gift would provide them, they may also qualify for the retirement savings tax credit.

Table 3.1 - Retirement Savings Credit - 2009 Limits			
Credit rate	Single, widow(er) or married separate filer income limits	Married, joint filer income limits	Head of household filer income limits
50%	Up to $16,000	Up to $32,000	Up to $24,000
20%	$16,001 to $17,250	$32,001 to $34,500	$24,001 to $25,875
10%	$17,251 to $26,500	$34,501 to $53,000	$25,876 to $39,750
No credit	$26,501 or more	$53,001 or more	$39,751 or more

Basically, the lower the income, the bigger the credit. Contributions to traditional and Roth IRAs as well as to 401(k) plans count toward computing the credit. In the case of the 401(k), only the employee contributions count, not any matching amounts the company contributed. The retirement savings credit is only available if the person files his or her own return and isn't claimed as a dependent on another person's tax return.

Roth Accounts as You Approach Retirement

You might hear the argument if you expect to be in a much lower tax bracket during retirement than you're in now, a tax-deductible IRA is a better deal than even a Roth IRA—especially if you're only a couple of years away from retirement. Some advisors say a contribution to a Roth must remain in the account for at least ten years to make it worthwhile; otherwise, the contribution won't have enough time to accumulate tax-free to offset the immediate benefit of the tax deduction. This would seem to make sense if you can take a tax deduction in the 25% tax bracket and expect to pay only 15% tax on the withdrawal.

Rick's Tip

A taxpayer eligible for the saver's credit could shave as much as $1,000 off his or her tax bill. This tax break is a credit instead of a deduction. Credits come into play after you calculate how much tax you owe the IRS and reduce your tax bill dollar for dollar. The actual credit amount depends on income, filing status, and the contribution amount to a retirement account.

However, there are a couple of fundamental problems with this philosophy. First, you're probably already overweighted in tax-deferred accounts, as most people are at retirement (that said, I'd be more inclined to go along with the philosophy if you're in the unusual position of having your three-legged stool overweighted in favor of the Roth). Second, it's unlikely you'll be drawing out this money early in your retirement. The contribution will probably have a few years of earnings before withdrawal, and time is on the Roth IRA's side, since time helps the account through tax-free compounding. Time works against you as the 2001 tax breaks are scheduled to expire at the end of 2010. It's possible, but not likely, the tax breaks will be extended, considering Congress' thirst for money.

Finally, you may retire to a lower tax bracket, but the taxation of Social Security benefits could put you into a higher "effective" tax rate. Social Security benefits aren't taxable until you reach a certain level of income. IRA distributions contribute to your income level and potentially make your Social Security benefits taxable. Let's assume you withdrawal $1,000 from your IRA. The withdrawal causes $500 of your Social Security benefit to become taxable. You pay 15% on the amount of the IRA withdrawal and 15% on the taxable portion of your Social Security benefits, for a total tax of $225 ($1,000 + $500 X 15%). That's an effective tax rate of 22½% on the IRA withdrawal (for a complete explanation of the taxation of Social Security benefits, see the forthcoming section on Understanding Social Security).

However, Roth IRA distributions don't add to the calculation for determining the taxation of Social Security benefits. This is also true for those who itemize deductions. Medical expenses and miscellaneous itemized deductions are both reduced by a percentage of your adjusted gross income. IRA distributions add to your adjusted gross income, which will reduce the amount of these deductions. Yet Roth IRA distributions don't add to adjusted gross income. Alternative minimum tax (AMT) is calculated off your net taxable income before personal exemptions, but Roth IRA distributions are not part of the net taxable income.

Rodgers' Recommendations for Roth Accounts

- Any year you have earned income that's low enough, you should make a Roth contribution.

- Make non-deductible IRA contributions when your income exceeds the limits, with the goal of converting them to Roth IRAs in 2010 (see the next section on Roth IRA Conversions for more detail on this topic).

- Both spouses can make Roth IRA contributions even if only one of them has earned income when the couple files a joint tax return.

- You can still make a Roth IRA contribution after you turn 70½ as long as you or your spouse has earned income.

ROTH IRA CONVERSIONS: BETTER THAN ANY TAX BREAK

The changes to the nation's tax system President Bush signed into law in May 2007 have a profound effect on the Roth IRA. The bill extends the dividend and capital gains tax cuts Congress first enacted in 2003, which set the maximum rate for both at 15%. While most of the attention has been focused on the amount of income exempted from the AMT, dividends, and capital gains, the Roth IRA conversion provisions could benefit you much more than any tax cuts.

Starting in 2010, if you earn $100,000 or more in adjusted gross income, you'll be allowed for the first time to convert your traditional IRA to a Roth IRA. To do this, you'd pay a large one-time tax payment, but then you'd be able to withdraw money from the account tax-free indefinitely. You wouldn't be forced to withdraw funds at age 70½ and could subsequently pass the money to your heirs in a more tax-advantageous way. Why do this? Because you don't have to pay tax on the earnings in your Roth IRA account when you withdraw the money.

Plus, the Roth IRA doesn't require you to take minimum distributions, as you're required to do with traditional IRAs starting at age 70½. These new provisions have the potential to wield significant influence on the millions of baby boomers who make over $100,000 a year.

Unlike the Bush tax cuts, the Roth IRA conversion provision is permanent. Some estimate a $6.4 billion income windfall to the government over the next ten years as baby boomers convert and pay income taxes on money withdrawn from traditional IRAs (spent or converted, either way, the government wins).

Under the new rules, the current income and contribution limits will continue to apply to Roth IRAs. Again, $5,000 a year can be contributed to accounts in 2009. If you're at least 50 years old, you can contribute an additional $1,000 a year. New contributions to a Roth IRA are limited to single taxpayers who make no more than $105,000 in adjusted gross income and to couples with a combined income of no more than $166,000. Partial contributions can be made for single filers with incomes between $105,000 and $120,000 and for joint filers with incomes between $166,000 and $176,000 in 2009. Those income limits are indexed for inflation.

The Roth IRA's highest value will be in the estate planning area; check out the section on Estate Planning with a Roth IRA for extended detail on this subject. For now, I'll give you the short story: If you're a high-net worth, self-employed person, you'll be able to move money from a "qualified" retirement savings plan such as a 401(k) into a Roth IRA. By paying income tax on your IRA funds in advance, the amount paid in income tax at the time of the conversion can be removed from your estate as the IRA holder. This will potentially lower the amount of tax that will have to be paid on your estate. This avoids the problem that the Richardsons, whom I talked about way back in the Introduction, had with their estate, when the amount of estate tax they paid could not be used to completely offset the income tax.

Rick's Tip

Beneficiaries of Roth IRAs must start taking distributions when they receive the accounts, but the distributions can be spread out over their life expectancies, and the money is income tax-free for them.

Now that you know the nuts and bolts behind Roth IRA conversions, how do you determine if this strategy is right for you? There's no easy answer to this question. Ultimately, each person must analyze this option based on their individual circumstances.

In general, *a conversion may be a good idea* if:

- You don't plan to touch the money in the Roth for at least the next five years.

- You can pay the income taxes due on the conversion without using funds from the traditional IRA when you convert.

- You expect to be in a higher tax bracket in future years. Paying the taxes now while you're in a lower income tax bracket should save you income taxes later.

- You don't expect to need money from the Roth IRA for income and want to build an estate for your heirs. In this case, the Roth IRA can minimize the overall income tax burden to the family; heirs get the proceeds free of income taxes, and in the interim, the proceeds can continue growing free of taxes.

- You don't expect to need income from your IRA, and you wish to avoid the annual mandatory distributions required from a traditional IRA when you reach age 70½.

- You believe current income tax rates are at the lowest level we'll ever see and Congress will most likely increase tax rates in the years to come.

A *conversion is generally a bad idea* if:

- You can't pay the income taxes due on the conversion without using funds from the traditional IRA. Taking tax from the conversion reduces the amount remaining within the Roth for compounding purposes. An early withdrawal penalty may apply for taking money from a traditional IRA before age 59½.

- The added income for the year caused by the conversion puts you in a significantly higher tax bracket (to avoid this, you can have your tax advisor calculate the amount of income you can add before moving into the next higher bracket, then only convert the amount that keeps you in your current tax bracket).

- You expect to be in a lower tax bracket in future years. Paying the taxes later at the lower rate would offset the lack of tax-free growth.

- You think Congress will adopt a radical change in the tax system whereby income will no longer be taxed. A national sales tax or some form of value added tax has been debated for years. Obviously, it wouldn't make sense to pay tax on income now if the income tax will be abolished in the future.

Rick's Tip

You may want to use some of the online calculators to help with your conversion decision. Vanguard has one of the most popular Roth conversion calculators on their website at www. vanguard.com. The calculator is free and easy to use.

Convert to Roth in Down Markets

The stock market meltdown from 2000 to 2002 caused many investors to lose faith in the financial markets, with good reason: the S&P 500 Index fell 49% from its peak in March 2000 to its low in October 2002. But for long-term investors holding stocks and stock funds in their retirement accounts, this was the perfect opportunity for a Roth conversion.

You'll have to pay taxes on the money you withdraw from your IRA account some day; what better time than when the market is down and you can pay tax on the discounted value? You'll still need to qualify for a Roth in 2009 by having an adjusted gross income of no more than $100,000. But as I mentioned in the last section, the income threshold will go away in 2010, when anyone will be eligible to do a conversion.

This strategy calls for some advance tax planning so you know you'll be able to qualify to do the conversion. Then, when the stock market goes into one of its sell-off periods, you'll be able to convert at the lower account value. If you're doing a partial conversion, you'll be able to convert more shares.

The big advantage of the Roth conversion strategy comes when the market recovers and the account grows back to its original value, since the account growth from the recovery will be all tax-free! (At least it will be, once you hold the funds for five years and have reached age 59½.) Check out the advantages to this strategy enjoyed by one of my clients, Jim Haller.

Case Study: Jim Haller, investor

In 2002, Jim Haller was still five years from retirement when the market entered its third year of the sell-off. He'd watched his 401(k) slip from $500,000 at the end of 1999 to $400,000 in mid-2002. His account was balanced between stocks and bonds; while the bonds helped offset some of the losses in the stocks, the IRA was still down 20% overall.

Like a lot of investors, Jim was overweighted in tax-deferred accounts. Most of his new savings were going into the 401(k) at work, which only added to his lop-sided savings. Now was the time to act if he was going to have any chance of obtaining a balanced three-legged stool for retirement.

After running some tax calculations together, Jim determined he could afford to pay the tax on a partial Roth conversion of $100,000. We chose only the stocks in his IRA to convert to the Roth and completed the conversion in August 2002. Six months later, as Jim was preparing to file his taxes, the market still hadn't recovered. We briefly considered undoing, or "recharacterizing," the Roth conversion before his filing deadline.

Rick's Tip

The process of undoing a Roth conversion is called a "Roth recharacterization." The IRS says it can be done until October 15 of the year following the year of the conversion. This rule exists because tax payers often don't know if they'll be able to stay under the $100,000 limit in earnings. You could easily add up all your W2s and 1099s in February only to find you earned too much money. A recharacterization allows you to put the money back into an IRA without paying tax or penalty. To recharacterize, the taxpayer must make a direct transfer of the funds from the Roth IRA back to a traditional IRA. The Roth conversion is now treated like it never happened.

If Jim had recharacterized, he wouldn't have had to pay the tax. If he'd recharacterized later in the year but before October 15, he'd get a refund by filing an amended tax return to get back the taxes he paid on value that no longer existed (this must be done for state tax returns as well). Another circumstance in which tax payers recharacterize a conversion is when they find the value they converted and paid tax on no longer exists due to a stock market decline. Jim was worried this is what would happen to him.

Jim chose to wait it out and paid the tax on his conversion. As it turned out, he ended up with a half-price sale. Five years later, the $100,000 Roth was worth $156,000. All of the growth he reclaimed was tax-free, and best of all, any future earnings would be tax exempt, too.

Fortunately, 46% drops in the stock market like the one from 2000 to 2002 are rare. However, 10-20% drops are a normal part of a stock market cycle. So when you hear the newscasters say "correction," think "conversion," since that means the stocks in your IRA are on sale—and you should take advantage of it.

Rodgers' Recommendations for Roth IRA Conversions

- Your adjusted gross income (not including the amount of the conversion) needs to be under $100,000 in 2009 in order to be eligible to convert your traditional IRA to a Roth IRA during those years. If you're making more than $100,000 by 2010, consider doing the conversion.

- The conversion will provide you with more flexible distribution capabilities since you can—but won't be forced to—start withdrawing money immediately.

- The same contribution rules will apply to converted Roth IRAs: $5,000 per year in 2009 ($6,000 if you're age 50 or older), and you must make less than $105,000 ($166,000 jointly for couples) in order to establish the account.

Before you convert an IRA to a Roth, make sure you know how much it will cost in taxes. You should have the money to pay the taxes in an account outside of the Roth.

Amateurs fear stock market corrections and try to time the market to avoid them. They usually end up buying high and selling low. Pros know corrections are part of the stock market's normal trading pattern and use them to take advantage of opportunities.

* * *

Our discussion about how to keep the IRS away from your retirement has now come full circle. With the knowledge you've gained about pre-tax, after-tax, and tax-free retirement savings strategies, you're well on your way toward establishing a personal plan that will keep you and your family comfortable long after you retire. In the next chapter, I'll tell you how to structure your plan so it strikes a good balance between these three strategies. We'll also talk about the most tax-efficient ways to withdraw your retirement savings, when it finally comes time to reap the rewards you've worked so hard to build. Finally, I'll give you tips on how to choose a smart financial advisor to help guide you through it all.

Chapter 4

Distributions: Strike an Ideal Balance Among All of Your Accounts

THE RETIREMENT DISTRIBUTION (R/D) FACTOR™

As we've discussed throughout this book, my Three-Legged Stool™ approach to retirement is based on balancing your savings between tax-deferred, after-tax, and tax-free accounts. Many (unwise) people today aren't concerned with balancing their savings. They simply save money in their company's 401(k) and spend everything else. When these people enter retirement, they'll have nothing but their tax-deferred savings to draw on.

This will be coming at a time when, I believe, the IRS will be even more aggressive in taxing these assets. Aggressive taxation goes against what we were originally told—that IRA and 401(k) accounts were created so we could defer income now until we retire and enter a *lower* tax bracket! It's likely just the opposite will happen; we may be seeing the lowest tax brackets *now*. The growing national debt and retiring baby boomers will probably put a greater strain on government finances in the future.

By determining your R/D Factor™ now, you can ensure you don't end up like the countless retirees who didn't balance their savings and pay the price in taxes. The R/D Factor (R/D = retirement distribution) is a measure of how well you've done with reducing your taxable retirement income by building a balanced three-legged stool. The scale runs from 0, the point at which all of your income is taxable, to 100, where all of your retirement income is tax-free. After you determine your R/D Factor, you can use it to create a balanced retirement plan if you don't already have one, or to rebalance your existing plan to ensure it will be tax-efficient upon your retirement.

The following example of my clients John and Mary Pritchard will give you an idea of how the R/D Factor works.

Case Study: John and Mary Pritchard, future retirees

John and Mary Pritchard have done what they think is a perfect job of saving for retirement by completely balancing their savings. By the time they retire, they expect to have $1 million in tax-deferred IRA/401(k) accounts; $1 million in their joint after-tax account; and $1 million in their Roth IRA tax-free accounts. Their total retirement savings of $3 million can be expected to distribute 4% ($120,000) per year based on the Trinity Study (I give more detail on this study in the next section).

To calculate the R/D Factor for the Pritchards, we assume 1/3 of their income will be drawn from each of the three sources.

Note the tax liability from the after-tax account isn't necessarily based on the amount of the withdrawal. The earnings in the after-tax account won't be taxed based on whether they're withdrawn or not. To estimate this amount, we assume the Pritchards have followed the allocation strategy explained in Leg Two of this book and only have stock funds in the after-tax account.

Table 4.1 - Calculating the R/D Factor			
Account Type	Total Income	Non-Taxable Portion	R/D Factor
Tax-Deferred Account	$ 40,000	$ 0	0
After-Tax Account	$ 40,000	$ 10,000	25
Tax-Free Account	$ 40,000	$ 40,000	100
Total	$120,000	$ 50,000	42

Even after following all the tax-efficient strategies I've explained in the book, there will be some tax implications from dividend distributions and rebalancing. A reasonable assumption is 1/3 of the return will be taxable each year. So assuming the after-tax accounts average 9%, then 3%, or $30,000, of their return will be taxable.

The Pritchards will be left with $70,000 in taxable income to report. If this was their only taxable income in 2008, and they filed a joint return, claiming only the standard deduction ($10,900) and personal exemptions ($3,500 each), they'd owe tax on $55,600. This amount would put them in the 15% bracket, meaning the tax bill would be about $8,000 on $120,000 of income. Not bad!

The R/D Factor™ for the Pritchards is 42 in this example, since 42% of their retirement income will be non-taxable. When they retire, they can adjust this factor if they want by changing the amount they'll distribute from the three accounts. They'll have a lot of flexibility with this until they reach the age of 70½ and have to start taking minimum distributions from the tax-deferred accounts.

Rick's Tip

A realistic objective is to aim for an R/D Factor™ of 50. This would provide a balance between tax planning for today and saving for retirement.

You should work with a knowledgeable tax advisor to develop strategies for using the R/D Factor to your advantage. In the example above, the Pritchards may want to withdraw more from the tax-deferred accounts when they retire, in order to maximize the 15% bracket. (The 2009 threshold for married filing jointly is $67,900 in taxable income.) And once they start drawing Social Security, they may want to increase their R/D Factor by taking more from the after-tax and tax-free accounts to minimize the amount of their Social Security benefits that are taxed. I explain this strategy in more detail in the forthcoming section on Social Security.

Why Not 100?

Again, my Three-Legged Stool™ approach to retirement planning is all about balance. Whenever I explain the strategy to audiences, someone usually asks me why we don't try to save everything in the tax-free accounts. Good question! True, saving everything in tax-free accounts would give you an R/D Factor™ of 100, and you wouldn't have to worry about retirement taxes. But there's a two-fold problem with making 100% tax-free savings your goal.

1. There are immediate tax benefits to using IRA and 401(k) accounts you don't want to ignore. Your annual tax planning should take into consideration the level of pre-tax savings that will keep you in a lower tax bracket. Itemized deductions are reduced on your total adjusted gross income (AGI). Alternative Minimum Tax (AMT) calculations are also based on your AGI.

Pre-tax savings accounts are often the only tool we have to minimize the AMT burden.

2. As you know from reading the Leg Three chapter, there are limits to putting money into a Roth IRA. Unless you have a Roth 401(k) offered through your employer, you may not even be able to contribute to a Roth if your income is too high. Even using these strategies, it would still be difficult to put 100% of retirement savings into a Roth without ignoring some significant tax issues.

Rodgers' Recommendations for the R/D Factor™

- The R/D Factor™ is the percentage of your retirement income that won't be taxable.

- Ideally, you should shoot for an R/D Factor of 50.

- When you retire, you should manipulate your R/D Factor™ to take maximum advantage of your tax situation each year, accelerating taxable income in low tax years and minimizing taxable income when needed to stay in a lower tax bracket.

- Balance is the goal—don't neglect to do tax planning today for a tax-free retirement later. Because tax laws change frequently, you want to take advantage of tax incentives now, since they may not be there down the road.

HOW AND WHEN TO TAKE RETIREMENT SAVINGS DISTRIBUTIONS

When it finally comes time to begin taking distributions from your retirement savings accounts, you'll be in an ideal position, since you will have balanced all of your accounts around your R/D Factor, which you determined long ago. The general rule of thumb about distributions is you withdraw money from your retirement accounts in the following order.

1. Taxable accounts (stocks and mutual funds)

2. Tax-deferred accounts (traditional IRAs and qualified plans)

3. Tax-free accounts (Roth IRAs)

The logic behind this order is: since you already paid taxes on the earnings from taxable accounts, there's no increased tax burden for spending the dividends and capital gains distributions. Therefore, withdraw from taxable accounts first.

Rick's Tip

When determining the taxes on capital gains, remember that for assets held longer than one year, taxable accounts are subject to the long-term capital gains rate, which is a maximum of 15% through 2010. Tax-deferred account distributions are treated as ordinary income and are subject to rates of up to 35%. Obviously, you should keep your assets in tax-free or tax-advantaged accounts as long as possible, because they continue to grow tax-deferred and potentially faster than a comparable investment in a taxable account.

Again, the way you take distributions from each of these accounts, and the way those distributions are taxed, are both determined by your age and investment type. First, let's talk about the four IRS-approved ways for calculating the annual distribution amount from an IRA.

Distributions from IRAs

Required Minimum Distribution (RMD)

RMD payments are calculated by dividing the account balance at the end of the year by the appropriate life-expectancy factor from one of three IRS life-expectancy tables—Uniform Lifetime, Single Life, or Joint and Last Survivor. To find the current RMD, divide the adjusted balance of all of your IRAs on December 31 of the previous year by the applicable divisor from the IRS Uniform Lifetime table below (which you can also find online at www.irs. gov). Be sure to use the age you'll be on this year's birthday. For example, if Joe turns 73 in December, find 73 on the table and use the appropriate factor to calculate his RMD—in this case, 24.7.

Table 4.2 - The IRS Uniform Lifetime Table					
Age	Applicable Divisor	Age	Applicable Divisor	Age	Applicable Divisor
70	27.4	80	18.7	90	11.4
71	26.5	81	17.9	91	10.8
72	25.6	82	11.1	92	10.2
73	24.7	83	16.3	93	9.6
74	23.8	84	15.5	94	9.1
75	22.9	85	14.8	95	8.6
76	22.0	86	14.1	96	8.1
77	21.2	87	13.4	97	7.6
78	20.3	88	12.7	98	7.1
79	19.5	89	12.0	99	6.7

If your spouse is the sole beneficiary of the IRA and is more than 10 years younger than you, you may use a separate IRS table—Joint and Last Survivor—which addresses actual joint life expectancy and will result in a lower RMD. If you die before the account is depleted, it will be passed to your designated beneficiary.

Rick's Tip

Keep in mind that once you start taking RMDs from retirement accounts, you can alter the distribution strategy accordingly, taking less from taxable accounts. You may also be able to stop paying estimated tax payments by electing to have taxes withheld from your RMD.

RMD Reminders

- The table used to calculate the first payment must be used for all future payment calculations.

- The RMD method is the only one that requires annual recalculation using the updated account balance and life-expectancy factor.

- The RMD method generally results in the lowest payment.

- IRS rulings provide an option for investors affected by depressed market conditions: Those using either the fixed amortization (the process of decreasing or accounting for an amount over a period of time) or fixed annuitization (the process of taking an asset and, by way of an installment sale or annuity sale, effectively converting the asset into a stream of payments) methods described below—both of which result in higher annual payments than the RMD method—may make a one-time change to the RMD method to avoid depleting their accounts.

Fixed Amortization

The account balance in the first year of payment is amortized using the investor's life-expectancy factor from IRS tables and a "reasonable" interest rate, which the IRS defines as not greater than 120%

of the federal mid-term rate for either of the two months immediately preceding the month in which payments begin.

The initial payment isn't recalculated once it's determined, and the payment amount remains the same each year.

Fixed Annuitization

This method is similar to the fixed amortization method, except the life expectancy factor—here called the annuity factor—comes from an IRS approved mortality table used in the life insurance industry, rather than from IRS tables.

The initial payment isn't recalculated once it's determined, and the payment amount remains the same each year.

72(t) Payments

Section 72(t) of the Internal Revenue Code, which imposes the 10% early withdrawal penalty on IRAs (I discuss this below), also allows specific types of penalty-free distributions—known as a series of substantially equal payments or 72(t) payments—prior to age 59½.

According to IRS rules, once the 72(t) payments have begun, no contributions, transfers, or rollovers into the IRA are permitted, and the 72(t) payment stream can't be modified (except for the one-time election to the RMD method discussed above). Any other modification would result in a 10% penalty, plus interest, on all payments made from the account to date.

If an investor needs to roll money into an IRA but has already begun 72(t) payments, a new IRA must be opened.

Next, I've included a breakdown of what will happen to each of your accounts should you attempt to withdraw money at certain ages.

IRA Distribution Age: Younger Than 59½

Unforeseen circumstances sometimes force you to dip into your retirement savings before the standard retirement age—59½. Should you decide to take retirement distributions before this age, the withdrawals will be considered "premature" and will be subject to certain penalties according to account type.

Traditional and SEP IRAs

If you're younger than 59½, any distribution from a traditional or Simplified Employee Pension (SEP) IRA is considered a premature distribution and is subject to ordinary income tax and a 10% penalty. However, there are exceptions to the 10% penalty, including:

- Rollover within 60 days
- Death
- Permanent disability as defined by the Internal Revenue Code
- Unreimbursed medical expenses in excess of 7.5% of your adjusted gross income
- Qualified higher education expenses
- Purchase, building, or rebuilding of a first home ($10,000 lifetime limit)
- Payment of medical insurance during a period in which you received unemployment compensation for at least 12 weeks
- Inheriting an IRA
- An IRS levy

- Distributions taken as a series of substantially equal periodic payments (72(t) payments)

SIMPLE IRAs

Savings Incentive Match Plan for Employees (SIMPLE) IRAs follow the same rules as traditional and SEP IRAs. However, during the first two years, a SIMPLE IRA is open: any premature distribution that doesn't qualify for one of the exceptions is subject to a 25% penalty, rather than 10%. It can only be rolled into another SIMPLE IRA, in which case, it will continue to be tax-deferred.

Roth IRAs

Though investors may withdraw their contributions at any time without tax or penalty prior to age 59½, any distribution of earnings is considered premature and is subject to a 10% penalty. Exceptions to the 10% penalty include:

- Unreimbursed medical expenses in excess of 7.5% of your adjusted gross income
- Qualified higher education expenses
- Payment of medical insurance during a period in which you received unemployment compensation for at least 12 weeks
- Inheriting an IRA
- An IRS levy
- Distributions taken as a series of substantially equal periodic payments (72(t) payments)

In addition, any earnings distributed from the account before it is five years old are subject to ordinary income tax. There are exceptions to both, however, including:

- Rollover within 60 days
- Death
- Permanent disability as defined by the Internal Revenue Code
- Purchase, building, or rebuilding of a first home ($10,000 lifetime limit)

See the forthcoming section on Tips for Taking an Early Retirement to find out more about how to maximize distributions before age 59½.

IRA Distribution Age: 59½ to 70½

At age 59½, distributions become qualified; that is, you no longer need to be concerned about the 10% premature distribution penalty. However, it's still important to understand the tax consequences of different IRA distributions.

Traditional, SEP, and SIMPLE IRAs

When you reach age 59½, distributions aren't subject to penalty but may be taxed as ordinary income. If you've made both deductible and nondeductible contributions to an IRA, the IRS will consider each distribution to be partially taxable and partially tax-free. IRS Form 8606 provides instructions for calculating the taxable portion.

Roth IRAs

Qualified distributions from a Roth IRA are those made after the five-year period beginning with the year the first contribution was made, and that meet one of the following criteria:

- The Roth IRA owner is age 59½

- The Roth IRA owner is disabled
- Payment is made to a beneficiary after the Roth IRA owner's death
- The Roth IRA owner is buying, building, or rebuilding a first home ($10,000 lifetime limit)

IRA Distribution Age: 70½ or Older

At 70½ years of age and older, distributions become required. The IRS forces IRA owners to begin taking distributions or else suffer the tax consequences, which break down as follows.

Traditional, SEP, and SIMPLE IRAs

Tax laws require that minimum distributions from an IRA begin no later than the required beginning date (RBD), or April 1 following the calendar year in which the IRA owner turns 70½. For example, if Alice turned 70 on March 12, 2005, and 70½ six months later on September 12, she must take her first required minimum distribution (RMD) no later than April 1, 2006. The April 1 rule is applicable only in the first year in which an RMD must be taken. In subsequent years, the deadline is December 31. Most people opt to take their first RMD by December 31 of the year they turn 70½ to avoid two taxable distributions in the same year. Returning to our example, if Alice waits until April 1, 2006, to take her first RMD, she'll have to take another minimum distribution by December 31, 2006, and both will be reported on her 2006 tax return. Failure to take any year's RMD will result in a 50% penalty on the amount that should have been withdrawn.

Roth IRAs

There are no required minimum distributions from Roth IRAs. However, your heirs will be required to make withdrawals upon your death.

Special Circumstances for Inherited IRAs

If you inherit an IRA, the account will be subject to different tax rules depending on whether the original owner passed away before or after the required beginning date (RBD) for taking distributions.

If the IRA owner passes away before the RBD, the following rules apply.

For a spouse beneficiary:
- Rollover the assets to her own IRA and assume ownership of them. She will then be subject to any applicable withdrawal penalties, including premature distribution penalties.

- Deplete the balance of the account by the end of the fifth year following the IRA owner's death.

- Take annual distributions based on her own life-expectancy factor as determined by the IRS Single Life table.

- Wait until the deceased would have reached his RBD, and then begin taking distributions based on the surviving spouse's life- expectancy factor.

For a non-spouse beneficiary:
- Deplete the balance of the account by the end of the fifth year following the IRA owner's death.

- Take annual distributions based on his own life-expectancy factor. Distributions must start in the year following the IRA owner's year of death. In subsequent years, the minimum distribution will be determined by the previous year's factor minus one.

For a non-individual beneficiary:
- Deplete the balance of the account by the end of the fifth year following the IRA owner's death.

The following rules apply if the *IRA owner passes away after the RBD*.

For a spouse beneficiary:
- Rollover the assets to her own IRA and assume ownership of them.

- Take annual distributions based on her own life-expectancy factor.

For a non-spouse beneficiary:
- Take annual distributions based on his own life-expectancy factor. Distributions must start in the year following the IRA owner's year of death. In subsequent years, the minimum distribution will be determined by the previous year's factor minus one.

For a non-individual beneficiary
- Take annual distributions based on the deceased's life-expectancy factor at death minus one—subtracting one for each subsequent year.

Distributions from Qualified Plans

To recap, distributions become qualified at age 59½, meaning they're no longer subject to the 10% premature distribution penalty. While all qualified plans must follow some basic rules set forth by the Employee Retirement Income Security Act (ERISA), many plans are customized. The following information is a general overview of distributions from qualified plans. If you're considering a qualified plan, be sure to ask for the Summary Plan Description (SPD) for it and study the distributions rules carefully.

Qualified Plan Distribution Age: Younger than 59½

Again, taking distributions from a qualified plan before you turn 59½ makes those distributions premature. Distributions made prior to age 59½ that aren't rolled over to another plan are generally subject to a 10% penalty. However, there are exceptions, including:

- Death
- Permanent disability as defined by the Internal Revenue Code
- Attainment of age 55 and separation from service
- Unreimbursed medical expenses in excess of 7.5% of your adjusted gross income
- Distributions made to a former spouse pursuant to a qualified domestic relations order
- 72(t) payments
- Financial hardship (if permitted by the plan)
- Plan termination without a successor plan named
- RMDs

- 24 months of accumulation and five or more years of participation

Qualified Plan Distribution Age: 59½ and Older

Distributions of elective deferrals are considered qualified plans only after age 59½.

Qualified Plan Distribution Age: 70½ and Older

In general, the same RMD rules that apply to IRAs apply to qualified plans.

Distributions Eligible for Rollover

No matter whether they come from an IRA or qualified plan, all distributions are eligible to rollover to another plan or IRA, except:

- Hardship withdrawals (when permitted by the plan)
- RMDs
- 72(t) payments after separation from service

Plans are required to withhold 20% from eligible rollover distributions that aren't directly rolled over. If a participant receives a distribution check and then decides to roll it into another plan, he or she must deposit the check into the new plan or IRA within 60 days of receiving it. To avoid taxes and penalties, the participant must pay out of pocket the amount of the 20% withheld by the plan before depositing the check. If not, the 20% will be subject to income tax—and a 10% penalty if the participant isn't yet 59½.

For example, if a retiree takes a $100,000 distribution from his former employer's 401(k) and requests the check be sent directly to him, the plan must withhold 20% and send him a check for $80,000. If he decides to roll his money into an IRA, he must contribute $20,000 of his own money to make up the amount withheld by his former employer. Otherwise, that $20,000 will be subject to income tax and, if the retiree is younger than 59½, a 10% premature distribution penalty.

Other Distribution Exceptions

In addition to the exceptions mentioned above, there are two other circumstances in which you may be permitted to take distributions without penalty.

In-service Withdrawals

Certain plans may allow participants to make distributions before they've experienced a triggering event, which is often called an "in-service withdrawal." Some plans may limit the availability of these in-service withdrawals to instances of financial hardship, while others may be more flexible in their requirements. Check the plan's SPD to determine if in-service withdrawals are permitted.

Loans

Some plans allow loans. The rules vary greatly from plan to plan, but in general, loans must not exceed 50% of the participant's vested balance or $50,000. The loan must generally be repaid in five years with at least quarterly payments. Longer repayment periods are allowed for loans used to purchase a primary residence.

Annual Withdrawal Rates: How Much Can You Afford?

You've spent years focusing on putting money into retirement savings, so you may not have given a lot of thought to taking money out when you retire. But spending your nest egg requires careful planning. Withdrawing too little money may mean you'll have to give up the lifestyle you were accustomed to before retirement. Taking out too much may deplete your savings too soon. So, how do you determine the withdrawal rate that works for you?

Before you answer this question, you should understand a few things:

- Both your withdrawal rate and your portfolio composition will have a significant impact on the longevity of your retirement savings.

- More conservative portfolios (those with 75-100% bonds) have not historically supported large withdrawal rates.

- The age at which you retire and your lifestyle in retirement should be considered when determining your withdrawal rate.

- Keep in mind that you will be required to begin taking distributions from most retirement plans once you reach age 70½.

Finding the Right Rate

In 1997, two economists at Trinity University in San Antonio, Texas, published a study in which they examined the probability of outliving savings. They based it on different withdrawal rates and different portfolio compositions over time. The results became known as the Trinity Study, which showed the critical factors affecting your savings are your asset allocation and your withdrawal rate. The following table is an updated version of that study.

Table 4.3 - The Trinity Study										
Annual withdrawal rate*	3%	4%	5%	6%	7%	8%	9%	10%	11%	12%
100% Stocks										
20 Years	0	2	3	5	7	13	23	35	45	48
30 Years	0	2	4	8	12	22	38	52	58	70
75% Stocks, 25% Bonds										
20 Years	0	0	0	3	5	10	25	42	50	57
30 Years	0	0	2	4	10	26	48	58	68	78
50% Stocks, 50% Bonds										
20 Years	0	0	0	0	3	10	33	50	63	78
30 Years	0	0	0	2	8	44	62	84	98	98
25% Stocks, 75% Bonds										
20 Years	0	0	0	0	0	25	65	75	83	87
30 Years	0	0	0	0	56	84	94	98	98	100
100% Bonds										
20 Years	0	0	0	3	45	55	72	82	88	90
30 Years	0	0	40	60	84	88	96	98	100	100

The percentages listed in Table 4.3 represent your chances of running out of money based on asset allocation and annual withdrawal rates. The results are historical, from December 25, 1935 to December 24, 2004 (note that past performance can't guarantee comparable future results, and historically, stocks are riskier investments than bonds).

Here's an example of how to use this information: if you had a portfolio with 75% stocks and 25% bonds, and you annually withdrew 7% of the initial value of the portfolio, there'd be a 5% chance you'd run out of money in 20 years and a 10% chance you'd run out of money in 30 years.

While asset allocation and withdrawal rate are important factors in retirement income planning, you'll also want to also keep the following in mind:

- **Age at retirement.** Early retirement means your savings must last longer. In addition, your annual Social Security benefit will be reduced if you begin collecting before the full-benefit age, which gradually increases to age 67 over the next few years.

- **Lifestyle.** Do you plan to maintain your current lifestyle in retirement? If so, you'll likely need about 70-80% of your current income. But every situation is different. Be realistic about your expenses.

- **Required minimum distributions (RMDs).** As you well know by this point in the book, most retirement plans require you begin taking minimum distributions at age 70½. You'll need to determine the required amount of the distribution you must take from your tax-deferred retirement plan and factor that amount into your overall withdrawal rate.

- **The unpredictable.** Basically, give yourself some financial wiggle room. Savvy income planning allows for factors you can't predict—and that aren't within your control. These include, for example, market volatility, your portfolio's performance relative to the overall market, inflation, or a change in personal circumstances. Build a cushion into your plan to help you weather these events.

Rick's Tip

Remember, seeking the help of a good financial advisor will help you determine the asset allocation and withdrawal rates that best suit your financial needs.

Rodgers' Recommendations for How and When to Take Retirement Savings Distributions

- Make sure you understand the IRS rules for taking money from your tax-deferred accounts. There are penalties for both taking money too soon and too late.

- When retiring before age 59½, you'll need to have a strategy in place to pull money from tax-deferred accounts and avoid the early withdraw penalties.

- SEP IRAs, SIMPLE IRAs, traditional IRAs, and Roth IRAs— they all have similar names, but their rules differ. Get advice from a qualified advisor if you aren't certain which plan you have and which rules apply.

- Pay attention to the deadlines when you're the beneficiary of an IRA or qualified plan. The choices you make could have huge tax implications if the deadlines aren't met.

TIPS FOR TAKING EARLY RETIREMENT

For many of us, early retirement is the Holy Grail of all the hard work and retirement planning we've done throughout our lives. In a recent survey of workers ages 30 to 50, more than half plan to retire at age 60 or younger, and only 6% plan to work past age 65[1].

---

1 Sandy Baker. *Your Complete Guide to Early Retirement: A Step-by-Step Plan for Making It Happen* (Atlantic Publishing Company, December 2007).

Yet even if the balances of your retirement accounts have reached a level that satisfies you, you're not out of the woods yet, since tax penalties for taking distributions from those accounts before the official retirement age of 59½ can drain the accounts quickly.

In this section, we'll talk about ways you can take an early retirement while avoiding some of the tax implications. Let's start out with a case study about Clair Williams, a client of mine who went about early retirement in the *wrong* way!

Case Study: Clair Williams, technology executive

Clair had always dreamed of taking early retirement, and at the end of 1999, she felt it was finally within her grasp. After working for a technology company for the past 10 years and investing aggressively, she had accumulated over $1 million in her company's 401(k). Clair worked for Lucent, and the company stock had been doing extremely well ever since it was spun off from AT&T.

Clair was 55 years old. Her pension would be small because she hadn't worked for Lucent very long, and there would be a penalty for retiring before age 59½. However, she calculated her 401(k) account had averaged over 20% per year. Clair knew she couldn't count on those high returns every year, but she thought just drawing 10% per year would provide over $100,000 a year.

Unfortunately the stock market peaked in early 2000—just two months after Clair retired. Technology companies like Lucent were hit especially hard. Clair had left her money in the company 401(k) because she could take distributions without an IRS penalty after age 55. She cut back on her distributions when the market started to decline, but she didn't cut back on her position in Lucent, since the company had been hit hard a couple of times in the past but had always bounced back. Clair felt if she could just ride it out, the stock would bounce back, and she'd be in good shape again. By the time she came in to see me in the middle of 2001, her 401(k) had shrunk to $400,000.

Retirement at the normal retirement ages of 62 or 65 is complex enough and requires good long-term planning. Taking early retirement—and for purposes of this section, we'll define this as any age under 59½—has twice the complexity. Dealing with tax penalties from retirement accounts, adding another 10 or more years to your life expectancy, and the health insurance issue are just some of the complexities that make early retirement extremely challenging. Yet by starting early and following the steps in this book, you may be able to achieve that goal and enjoy a comfortable lifestyle. You can begin with three important steps.

Three Steps to Start Your Early Retirement Planning

Step 1: Start Preparing Early

The sooner you retire, the less time you have to save. In addition, you'll need to withdraw money from your accounts sooner, which means it will have to last longer. You won't be saving anything after retirement, because you have no earned income.

Your strategy should be to save as much as you can as early as you can while you're still working. My Three-Legged Stool™ approach is still the right model even for early retirement, so you want to be accumulating in all three types of savings. The more you contribute now, the more your money may compound and grow for the time you need it. And the more it grows, the longer it may last.

Rick's Tip

Step 2: Determine How Much You Plan to Spend

Think about the type of life you want to lead after you stop working, then figure out how much your present lifestyle costs you and compare the two costs. You'll probably find some things will cost less in retirement while others will cost more. For example, will you be playing more golf? Traveling more?

Another significant consideration will be your long-term health care costs. Medicare benefits generally don't begin until age 65, and it's not a good idea to go without health coverage until age 65 if you retire early: a serious illness or injury could potentially wipe out your life savings. If you need to obtain private medical insurance before age 65, start by checking with your employer to find out if health coverage for retired employees is available.

Rick's Tip

You'll also need to factor in the effect of inflation on your retirement expenses. A 3½% inflation rate will double your expenses in

20 years. What you budget to maintain your lifestyle at age 55 will cost twice that at age 75 and will be three times as much at age 87.

Step 3: Determine How Much You Need to Accumulate in Savings

In general, you'll need enough money to take a 4% withdrawal and meet your budgeted expenses. For example, if your budget calls for spending $100,000 per year, you'll need to accumulate $2½ million in savings, and 4% of $2½ million is $100,000. This assumes you'll have no other sources of income, which is very likely when you retire before age 59½. Some companies that offer pensions will allow early retirees to access their pension at a discount.

Once you reach age 62, you'll be eligible to start drawing your Social Security benefits unless Congress changes the rules again. You can use your expected benefits to reduce your monthly benefits when calculating the amount of savings you need. Going back to the earlier example of $100,000 needed for expenses, let's assume Social Security will pay $20,000 per year at 62. Your investments will need to support the balance of $80,000, so you'll need to accumulate $2 million in savings to support those distributions.

Be aware the benefit estimate you receive from Social Security assumes you intend to work up the point you start drawing and your earned income will be the same. Retiring earlier than 62 could alter those figures. You'll need to read the Understanding Social Security section to determine the impact early retirement will have on your estimated benefits.

After you've done all the number crunching and determined you can afford to retire early, where will the money come from? The strategy for using the new three-legged stool is the same. However, there are some very important penalty situations to work around until you reach age 59½.

You may think early retirement is a wonderful thing. However, the IRS doesn't agree. As I mentioned earlier, the U.S. tax code generally deems age 59½ to be the earliest anyone should retire. You could face ugly tax bills when accessing tax-deferred retirement accounts. You'll almost certainly pay federal income tax, and you may even be subject to state income taxes in states that don't normally tax retirement income. Most importantly, there's a 10% premature-withdrawal penalty that needs to be addressed. It's not always possible to get around this penalty, but by planning your strategy around the following three methods, you can avoid it.

Three Methods for Avoiding the Premature-Withdrawal Penalty

Roth IRA Withdrawals

You know from reading the section on Roth IRAs that these accounts allow you to withdraw the money you contributed without penalty. Because all contributions to a Roth are made with after tax dollars, there are no federal income taxes on the withdrawals, because they are considered a return of your principal. The trick is in making sure you're only withdrawing contributions, because the money in your Roth can potentially come from three different sources: your annual after-tax contributions; conversions of traditional IRAs to Roth IRAs; and the investment earnings on either your contributions or conversions.

Roth IRA distributions are considered to come from these three sources in the order listed above. The tax rules to withdrawals from these sources are as follows:

- **Annual Contributions:** You can withdraw contributions income tax-free and penalty-free at any time. For the early retiree, this is a readily accessible source of cash.

- **Conversions:** You can not touch this money within five years of the date of conversion, or you will owe the 10% premature-withdrawal penalty. The tax was already paid on the principal, but you avoided the premature withdrawal penalty when you transferred the money directly from the IRA to the Roth. Conversion money is only a good source of cash if the funds have been in the Roth for at least five years.

- **Earnings:** Withdrawals before age 59½ will be subject to federal income taxes and even state income taxes in some states. You'll also be assessed the 10% premature-withdrawal penalty tax, unless you qualify for an IRA penalty exception described in Leg Two under tax-deferred accounts. You should only draw earnings from your Roth IRA as a last resort.

Company Plans & 401(k)s

The standard 10% premature-withdrawal penalty applies to IRAs for those under age 59½. But the penalty is waived for withdrawals from company plans and 401(k)s once you reach age 55. This is an important planning consideration for an early retiree. You need to check with your employer to determine what they'll allow you to do with these funds after you retire. Many employers won't permit periodic distributions, since in that case, the employer will continue to be responsible for reporting distributions and balances to the IRS. It's generally to their advantage to get you to take your funds and move on. Consider the following case study about my client, Audrey Kaufman.

Case Study: Audrey Kauffman, corporate executive

Audrey Kauffman wanted to retire at age 56 so she could be available to help care for her elderly mother. After reviewing her financial needs and running projections, we determined Audrey would need a total of $140,000 for the next 3½ years to supplement her pension and annuity payments. This put her in the early-retirement ballpark, though she faced a major obstacle: nearly all of her savings were in the company 401(k) account.

Audrey had already put all of her after-tax savings toward a college education for her two sons. She was eligible to begin drawing the company pension immediately, and she had a non-qualified tax-deferred annuity we were able to annuitize, which would supplement her income. Still, these sources combined would only provide about half of the income she'd need to get her to age 59½.

We checked with her employer's policies on distributions from the 401(k) plan for retirees and found Audrey only had two options: she could leave it in the plan untouched until she reach age 70½; or she had to take it all out at once. We could rollover the entire 401(k) to an IRA and start taking 72(t) distributions, which would avoid the penalty. The problem with this strategy was she'd be locked into it for five years, and she only needed to bridge 3½ years to get to age 59½.

Looking closer at the plan, we discovered Audrey had $25,000 in after-tax contributions in her 401(k). Those funds would be separated from the rest and paid to her without tax or penalty when the 401(k) was rolled over. We also found she had $75,000 in company stock that had a low cost basis, which made it attractive for the NUA strategy I described in Leg One.

Based on all of this information, Audrey decided to take the following steps:

- Do a full distribution of the 401(k) for 100% of the cash and none of the company stock.

- Split the distribution, with $50,000 going to Audrey and the balance going to her IRA.

- Distribute the company stock to her directly in-kind.

The full distribution of the 401(k) generated four checks: $25,000 to Audrey for the after-tax contributions; $50,000 to Audrey with 20% withheld for taxes (net to Audrey = $40,000); $10,000 to the IRS for the tax withholding; and a check for the balance made payable to her IRA custodian. She received a stock certificate for the company stock about two weeks later.

All together, she had checks for $65,000 and a stock certificate worth $75,000. The transaction had an R/D Factor of 35 with no tax penalties. As long as she did a good job budgeting the funds, we projected that they would last her through age 59½, when she could begin taking distributions with no penalty.

72(t) Payments

72(t) payments, which we talked about earlier, are generally the surest way to make yourself eligible for penalty-free retirement account withdrawals before age 59½. To implement these payments in your early retirement strategy, simply follow these three basic rules.

1. You must take a series of withdrawals (at least annually) with the amounts based on one of three methods we discussed in

the last chapter: minimum distribution, fixed amortization, or fixed annuitization.

2. With a company plan or 401(k), you must be separated from service. That means you must have quit, retired, been laid off or fired, or otherwise left your job. With a traditional or Roth, SEP, or SIMPLE IRA, you can use the 72(t) strategy at any time.

3. Once you start taking 72(t) withdrawals, you must stick with the program for at least five years or until you reach age 59½, whichever comes later. You can't modify the account or payments in any way. To do so will subject all payments taken under the plan to the 10% premature withdrawal penalty.

The following case study about my client Sam Johnson demonstrates the value of using the 72(t) method.

Case Study: Sam Johnson, early retiree

Sam Johnson took early retirement and set up 72(t) distributions from his IRA rollover account. His wife was ten years younger and still working. She added Sam to her company's medical insurance plan and planned to cover him until he was eligible for Medicare. Three years later, Sam's wife was laid off from her job. She'd worked for a small employer that wasn't required to offer COBRA coverage. Sam was concerned that neither of them would have medical coverage. He called his former employer, who offered him his job back immediately with full benefits.

Sam no longer needed the 72(t) distributions, but he knew he was required to keep taking them. He decided to start putting money into the company 401(k) again to offset the income from his IRA. However, the next enrollment period wasn't until the following year. His accountant told him he was eligible to make a deductible IRA contribution, so he did. Unfortunately, he put it in the same IRA account from which he was taking 72(t) distributions. The three years of distributions now all became subject to the 10% premature withdrawal penalty.

What Sam didn't know is you may have several IRA accounts and only take 72(t) distributions from one of them. What I usually do is take the amount of income the client wants, then determine what the account balance needs to be that will generate that amount. For example, a client who's age 55 wants $1,000 per month from his IRA. Using the fixed amortization method and the single life expectancy table, the client needs to have $198,575 in his IRA. For this type of client, I'll split his IRA into two separate IRAs. One will hold $198,575 and the other will contain the remaining balance. The 72(t) will be taken from the first IRA. If the client decides to make an IRA contribution later on, like Sam Johnson did, he can add it to the second IRA account without disturbing his 72(t) account. Should he decide $1,000 per month isn't enough, he could divide the second account again and start another 72(t) distribution.

Rick's Tip

If you go through all the recommended steps and determine you can retire early, do you know what you'll do with your time? I can tell you many stories of clients who retired in their 60s and were bored after a year. When you start making a financial plan to retire early, start planning what you're going to do with your time when that day comes. Make sure you have something to do and look forward to before you retire— at any age!

Taking the chance of retiring early is a big risk. Early retirement requires a long-term savings and investing plan, and it takes discipline. This means keeping debt down and perhaps not living as lavishly now, so you can reap the benefits later. If you start planning early in life and do your homework, early retirement may be for you.

Finally—and this is critical—seek a competent, experienced financial planner to double-check your own numbers. As you'll learn more about in the next section, this planner can serve as a sounding board to give you a second opinion about your retirement strategy and investment allocations. After all, you'll hopefully only plan for retirement once, so you need to do it right! An experienced planner has probably helped hundreds of people retire and knows what to look for or when something might be out of place. An experienced planner would have, for example, advised Clair Williams to keep working, because a 10% withdrawal rate was too high. Had she kept her job, she would've been able to ride out the stock market drop and would probably be retired today. Instead, she'll be working at least part-time well into her 70s.

Rodgers' Recommendations for Taking Early Retirement

Use realistic rates of return for your projections and the safe withdrawal rates from the Trinity Study to determine if you have enough savings to retire.

Early retirement requires disciplined savings and careful planning. Start early. You'll need to accumulate more money in a shorter period of time.

Employers have a lot of flexibility in setting the rules for how their plans work. Make sure you know the rules for distributions from your employers' plan. You don't want to take an early retirement only to find out you can't get to the money in your company plan.

The IRS doesn't like people taking early retirement. They've set up road blocks to keep you from getting to your retirement funds. Make sure you have adequate after-tax savings if you're planning to retire early so you don't fall into one of the IRS' tax traps.

GET GUIDANCE FROM A GOOD FINANCIAL ADVISOR

One of the biggest dangers people face when planning for retirement is knowing how to differentiate good financial advice from bad. The following case study about retirees Walter and Bernice Kimball demonstrates what can happen if you don't take the time to seek out the right advice before you retire.

Case Study: Walter and Bernice Kimball, retirees

Walter and Bernice Kimball had dreamed of retiring at age 65 so they could travel and pursue their hobbies. They didn't get a lot of guidance from financial advisors throughout their lives, thinking instead that being good savers was enough. They continued to participate in their employers' 401(k) plans for their entire professional lives. The Kimballs also set a little money aside in after-tax accounts, and after Bernice received an inheritance of $250,000 in the 1990s, she put this money away for retirement, too.

The Kimballs sought advice from an advisor about how to invest Bernice's inheritance. The advisor sold them a variable annuity, explaining the earnings would be tax-deferred and the principal was guaranteed. The Kimballs invested the entire inheritance amount in the annuity.

Had the advisor been following my Three-Legged Stool™ strategy for retirement, he would have seen the Kimballs were already overweighted in tax-deferred accounts. They should have invested the inheritance after-tax and used the earnings to fund Roth IRAs for both of them each year.

Finally, the Kimballs turned 65 and had accumulated $1 million in their various retirement accounts, savings they felt made them ready to retire and enjoy the fruits of their hard work. Yet since the majority of these savings was in their tax-deferred 401(k) plans, the Kimballs' overall retirement picture was not quite as rosy as it appeared.

Unfortunately, Walter and Bernice soon learned $1 million before taxes isn't the same as $1 million after taxes. Their retirement spending plan required an after-tax cash flow of $5,000 per month. Social Security would provide $2,500 per month, so the balance had to come from investments. They had $100,000 in joint savings, $300,000 in the non-qualified variable annuity, and $600,000 in the 401(k) plans that had been rolled over to IRA accounts.

They decided not to touch the joint savings, so it would be available for emergencies or for large purchases they may need to make in the future. The $2,500 would come from either the annuity or IRAs, but either way, it would be taxable as ordinary income.

To complicate matters, the tax laws state that taking $30,000 in ordinary income makes part of your Social Security taxable, resulting in a tax bill of about $2,000, putting Walter and Bernice in the ugly tax bracket where part of their Social Security would be taxed. So, increasing their annual income by $1,000 would actually increase taxable income by $1,500 or more.

The Kimballs' IRA funds could be withdrawn in a lump sum in one year, which would expose 85% of their Social Security to tax in just one year instead of spreading it out over several years. However, they'd pay a higher tax rate on most of the withdrawal. The money would be invested in an after-tax account, generating taxable income that could make their Social Security benefits taxable anyway.

Clearly, the Kimballs needed help rethinking their retirement savings plan before they could reach their goals. They finally sought out a good financial advisor who redirected their plan in a much more tax-efficient direction.

To start, the advisor recommended the couple capitalize on the better option of annuitizing their variable annuity. Again, annuitization is the process of taking an asset and, by way of an installment sale or annuity sale, effectively converting the asset into a stream of payments. Bernice would surrender her policy to the insurance company in exchange for a stream of payments called a payout option.

Rick's Tip

Some payout options guarantee income for as long as you live, while other options spread your distribution out over the number of years you choose. Guaranteed lifetime options include life income only, life income with a guaranteed number of payments, and joint life payments. Non-lifetime options include payments for a fixed number of years or payments of a specified amount. You choose the form of distribution when you're ready to begin receiving payments, and this decision is irrevocable.

Bernice chose to annuitize her contract over 10 years, during which she'd receive 120 payments of $2,900 each. $806 of each payment would be considered interest and taxed as ordinary income, while $2,094 of each payment would be considered a return of principal and wouldn't be taxed or used in the calculation to determine the taxability of her Social Security. If she were to die before the 10 years were completed, the payments would continue to her designated beneficiary.

This change made Walter and Bernice's income tax projection completely different. Less than $10,000 per year of the annuity payment became taxable, so none of their Social Security benefits would be subject to tax. The standard deduction and personal exemptions would shelter the annuity income, resulting in a zero tax liability.

Fortunately, the Kimballs' new advisor wasn't short-sighted enough to stop the strategy there, since the annuity payments would end in 10 years, and the couple would simply be faced with the same problem all over again. In five years, both Walter and Bernice would turn 70½ and would need to start taking withdrawals from their IRAs to meet the required minimum distribution (RMD). They'd need to take advantage of the tax situation they created and continue to pull money from the tax-deferred accounts.

Each year, the couple decided to convert $17,000 of their IRAs to Roth IRAs. Converting this amount would make $3,800 of their Social Security benefits subject to tax. After claiming the standard deduction and personal exemptions, their taxable income would only be $13,000 and would be taxed at the 10% rate. Therefore, their strategy for the next five years was changed to convert the maximum amount from their rollover IRAs to Roth IRAs and stay in the 10% tax bracket. Their rollover IRAs would still likely grow, even with the conversions. At 6% per year, the IRAs would grow to $700,000, and their first year RMD would be $25,600 (note RMDs aren't eligible for conversion to Roth IRAs). The Roth IRAs would probably grow to $100,000 in the same period of time.

Walter and Bernice accomplished several important objectives at the end of their five year strategy. First, they produced their monthly income goal of $5,000 in a very tax-efficient manner. Second, the Roth conversions slowed the growth of their rollover IRAs so their RMD became $25,600. This figure is $3,600 less than it would have been without the Roth conversion. Lastly, they built up a $100,000 tax-free source of funds. Should they need a lump sum of money to buy a car or take an extravagant vacation, they could now choose to withdraw from the joint savings or the Roth, depending on the tax implications.

This complicated problem was dealt with after the Kimballs were ready to retire. Had they hired a good financial advisor to help them map out a solid plan long *before* retirement, they could have avoided the whole mess.

Great idea, you're probably thinking, *but how on earth do I find a good advisor*? The answer to this question is compounded by the entry of new players into the business of advice drawn by the immense revenue opportunities available today.

Unless you understand the difference between advisors and planners, you'll likely be disappointed and lose faith in the entire industry. Beware many financial planners today are salespeople in advisors' clothing. This indictment includes some stockbrokers, insurance salesmen, and tax advisors who have changed their titles to "financial planner." Often these individuals desire to sell products. There's little regulation in this area, and most individuals who call themselves financial planners aren't licensed. Of the 25,000 financial planners in the State of California alone, less than 5% are registered with the California Department of Corporations.

Studies confirm individuals managing their own money tend to lack discipline, and those working with financial planners, who are often commission brokers, aren't doing much better. That's because individuals working with a financial planner or stockbroker are adding value only in one dimension. While it's true a broker can help individual investors by providing some discipline, the tools they're using are inappropriate for developing an overall strategy.

It's critical for investors to find an advisor who understands asset class investing and utilizes this latest tool previously available only to the largest pension plans. Often investors and inexperienced advisors believe once they build an asset class portfolio, they won't need to make any changes. Yet if we look back only five years, we can see asset class investing has improved dramatically. Over the next five years, it's likely we'll see even greater changes. It would be foolish for any investor not to take advantage of this enormous opportunity. Finding an advisor to help utilize asset class investing and stay abreast of any new improvements will add tremendous value to that investor's portfolio.

Rick's Tip

DALBAR has taken one step toward helping consumers understand the advice offerings available through a consumer booklet entitled ADVICE, TRUST & MONEY. This booklet outlines four categories of advice services available today and compares key features of each. It's being distributed to consumers by members of the advice community and is available free online at www.DALBAR.com.

Rodgers' Recommendations for Finding the Right Advisor

When you interview potential new advisors, bring along the following list of key questions—and expect the following answers:

- **What's your professional background? Certified Financial Planner (CFP)? Licenses? Training? Credentials? (Remember to verify all answers after the meeting.)** Preferred registrations and licenses include:

    - Certified Financial Planner® or Chartered Financial Counselor

        ◦ Personal Financial Specialist (PFS)

        ◦ Registered Investment Advisor

        ◦ NAPFA Registered Investment Advisor

        ◦ MS Personal Financial Planning

- **How long have you been in the community and in this business?** Both the CFP Board and NAPFA require a minimum of at least three years of qualifying full-time work experience for certification.

- **Are you registered with the SEC and/or your state's Department of Corporations?** The advisor should answer yes to both questions.

- **Who will I be dealing with—you personally, or one of your associates?** Obviously, getting your advice directly from the source is preferable to being handed off to one of the advisor's junior associates. Don't settle for less than the advisor's personal attention.

- **Can you provide me with references?** Ask for references to clients that have similar circumstances to your own situation—preferably clients who retired from the same company you work for currently. If the advisor has had clients who retired from your employer, he or she will be familiar with your company's retirement plan and benefits. Ask for new clients as well as clients that have been with the advisor for several years.

- **Will you be giving me a written contract?** The agreement should clearly spell out how the advisor will be compensated and give the conditions for which the agreement can be terminated. You should also be given a current copy of the firm's ADV part II. This form is like a prospectus on an advisory firm and explains potential conflicts of interest.

- **What tasks will you perform?** At a minimum, a good financial advisor should:

  - Work with you to determine your time horizon for investing. No one should ever invest without at least a five-year time horizon. Even for retirees, a five-year or longer horizon fits most situations.

  - Remind you there will be down years; and he or she should help you maintain an investment position that permits you to ride through those years without losing sleep.

  - Help you set target rates of return and structure the investment strategy in a way so that the return of the entire investment portfolio can achieve your objectives with the least amount of risk.

- Write out a financial plan with you (I go into more detail about written financial plans in Appendix). This plan should be very specific and cover topics such as: target rates of return, risk tolerance, anticipated withdrawals or contributions, and desired holding periods.

- Rebalance your plan periodically. If an asset differs by more than 5% from its original target allocation, then he or she should either buy more or sell some of the assets until the target percentage is restored. The advisor should look frequently at your overall balance, especially when the financial markets are setting new highs.

- Provide some method of measurement and measure your investment performance quarterly. He or she should determine, by using time-weighted rates of return, whether the market value of the portfolio is growing fast enough to achieve your target objective.

- Highlight the advantages of lower volatility, high relative returns, and why a particular manager's performance is leading or lagging the market. These are key elements in identifying a trend and getting in front of it. This goes way beyond just identifying the managers who have had exceptionally good performance near-term.

- When making a mutual fund selection, or when contemplating the termination of a mutual fund, the advisor must look at how long a manager's performance has been lagging behind market averages and/ or their peer group averages. Keep in mind the market average is a compilation of all the different stocks that fall into every one of the management disciplines. The certain segments which will be leading will actually be the ones that are influencing the averages.

- **How will you be paid? By whom?** Advisors should be compensated on a fee-only basis rather than by brokerage commissions. Advisors who work on commission aren't held to a fiduciary standard. They're not required to put your interests first, nor do they have to disclose conflicts of interest. In contrast, a fee-only advisor has a more objective position and is more likely to follow one of the modern investment strategies.

* * *

We've covered a lot of ground about retirement plans, but there's one big topic we haven't yet tackled: Social Security. Pick up a newspaper on any given day, and you're likely to encounter at least one story about how this traditional retirement plan is in big trouble. In the next section, I'll help you understand the origins of this government-sponsored retirement approach and how to access your share in a tax-efficient way. In addition, we'll cover the problems Social Security faces today and how we can go about getting the system back on the right track.

Chapter 5

Understanding Social Security

SOCIAL SECURITY: A HISTORY

Most people think of Social Security as just a retirement plan, but it was actually designed to function as insurance against the loss of income due to retirement, disability, and the loss of a wage earner (survivor benefits).

Today, about 98% of all workers are in jobs covered by Social Security. Over 54 million people—one-sixth of the population—receive monthly Social Security, or SSI, benefits, according to the 2007 Social Security Administration's Performance and Accountability Report.

Rick's Tip

In the fiscal year 2007, the program took in $802 billion and disbursed $629 billion. It's a huge program that has grown to become an essential part of modern life and has been modified to provide for widows, orphans, the disabled, and divorced spouses. It will only grow larger as the baby boom generation begins to retire and the government struggles to come up with a way to pay their promised benefits.

According to the Social Security website, Social Security benefits already comprise about 5% of the nation's total economic output. So, how did this enormously important program come to be? The website[1] estimates over half of the elderly in America had insufficient income during the Great Depression. Many states enacted legislation to provide some form of old-age pension, but these programs proved to be inadequate, and 18 states had no program whatsoever by 1935. On August 14 of that year, President Roosevelt signed the Social Security Act into law. The new Act provided a nationwide retirement and social welfare program for the first time. This program was designed to pay retired workers age 65 or older a continuing income after retirement.

We can never insure one hundred percent of the population against one hundred percent of the hazards and vicissitudes of life, but we have tried to frame a law which will give some measure of protection to the average citizen and to his family against the loss of a job and against poverty-ridden old age.

—President Roosevelt, upon signing the Social Security Act

The new Act contained two major parts: Title 1, which supplemented the state welfare programs for the elderly; and Title 2, which is the program we know today as Social Security. Originally, benefits were paid only to the primary worker based on payroll tax contributions made during the worker's life. Payroll taxes began in 1937, and benefits started in 1942.

How the system works today is, throughout your career, you pay a portion of your wages to Social Security in the form of pay-

1   U.S. Social Security Administration, Historical Background and Development of Social Security, http://www.socialsecurity.gov/history/briefhistory3.html (March 2003).

roll taxes (FICA). Your employer contributes an equal amount. If you're self employed, you pay both the employee and employer portion. In return, you receive certain benefits that can provide income to you when you need it, either at retirement or when you become disabled. Your family members can receive benefits based on your earnings record, too. The amount of benefits you and your family members receive depends on several factors, which we'll talk about in the next section.

Rodgers' Recommendations for Understanding Social Security

Make sure the Social Security Earnings statement you receive periodically is accurate. You should be receiving one of these statements annually, about three months before your month of birth. The statement is your personal record of the earnings you paid Social Security taxes on during your working years. The statement goes on to estimate the benefits you and your family may receive as a result of those earnings. The statement is important in several ways:

1. The benefit estimates play an important role in your financial planning. Social Security benefits combine with your investments, pensions, and retirement accounts to make up your retirement income.

2. It ensures your earnings are correct on your record. Any mistakes should be reported and corrected promptly. The sooner you identify mistakes, the easier it will be to get the Social Security system to correct them.

3. The information in your statement is a record of the protection you've earned under Social Security for your family members should you become disabled or die before you reach retirement

age. A copy should be kept with your estate planning documents.

HOW YOUR BENEFITS ARE CALCULATED

There are three components to determining your Social Security benefit—eligibility, average earnings, and age. Let's look at each one in detail.

Three Factors in Social Security Benefits

Eligibility

To be eligible for benefits, a worker needs to be employed and subject to Social Security taxes for 40 quarters. Each quarter you work earns you one work credit. Eligibility is based on the number of work credits you have. You need 40 work credits to be eligible to receive retirement income benefits if you were born in 1929 or later. People born before 1929 need fewer than 40 credits; fewer work credits are also required to receive disability benefits based on your age. A fully insured status enables the worker to receive unrestricted retirement, disability, and survivor payments. You earn a maximum of four credits in one year by working and paying Social Security taxes. Credits are based on your total wages (and/or self-employment income) during the year. In 2009, you must earn $1,090 in covered earnings to get one work credit and $4,360 to get the maximum four credits for the year.

Average Earnings

Social Security must first compute a worker's benefit by adjusting all of the earnings over their working life to reflect the change in general wage levels. Indexing ensures the worker's benefit will reflect the rise in the standard of living that has occurred during their working lifetime. Social Security will use the highest 35 years of earnings going back to 1951 to compute the average indexed monthly earnings (AIME). I've included the national average wage indexing series chart below.

Table 5.1 - National Average Wage Indexing Series, 1951-2006					
Year	Index	Year	Index	Year	Index
1951	2,799.16	1971	6,497.08	1991	21,811.60
1952	2,973.32	1972	7,133.80	1992	22,935.42
1953	3,139.44	1973	7,580.16	1993	23,132.67
1954	3,155.64	1974	8,030.76	1994	23,753.53
1955	3,301.44	1975	8,630.92	1995	24,705.66
1956	3,532.36	1976	9,226.48	1996	25,913.90
1957	3,641.12	1977	9,779.44	1997	27,426.00
1958	3,673.80	1978	10,556.03	1998	28,861.44
1959	3,855.80	1979	11,479.46	1999	30,469.84
1960	4,007.12	1980	12,513.46	2000	32,154.82
1961	4,086.76	1981	13,773.10	2001	32,921.92
1962	4,291.40	1982	14,531.34	2002	33,252.09
1963	4,396.64	1983	15,239.24	2003	34,064.95
1964	4,576.32	1984	16,135.07	2004	35,648.55
1965	4,658.12	1985	16,822.51	2005	36,952.94
1966	4,938.36	1986	17,321.82	2006	38,651.41
1967	5,213.44	1987	18,426.51		
1968	5,571.76	1988	19,334.04		
1969	5,893.76	1989	20,099.55		
1970	6,186.24	1990	21,027.98		

Insured workers become eligible for retirement benefits when they reach age 62. If 2008 were the year of eligibility, Social Security would divide the national average wage index for 2006 ($38,651.41) by the national average wage index for each year prior to 2006 in which the worker had earnings, then multiply each such ratio by the worker's earnings. This would give the indexed earnings for each year prior to 2006. Wages earned in or after 2006 at face value would be used at face value. If a worker didn't have 35 years of earnings, a zero would be entered for those years to reach a total of 35.

Once AIME is determined, then the primary insurance amount (PIA) is used to determine the benefit. PIA is the benefit a worker would receive if he or she elected to begin receiving retirement benefits at his or her normal retirement age. This benefit amount is neither reduced for early retirement nor increased for delayed retirement.

The PIA is the sum of three separate percentages of portions of AIME. The portions depend on the year in which a worker attains age 62. In 2009, the portions are the first $744, the amount between $744 and $4,483, and the amount over $4,483. These dollar amounts are the "bend points" of the 2009 PIA formula. The bend points in 2009 are as follows:

- 90% of the first $744 of average indexed monthly earnings, plus

- 32% of average indexed monthly earnings over $744 and through $4,483, plus

- 15% of average indexed monthly earnings over $4,483.

The resulting benefit amount can be affected by the final component of calculation—age.

Age

Be aware if you were born before 1938, you'll be eligible for full Social Security retirement benefits at age 65, but if you were born in 1938 or later, the age at which you're eligible for full retirement benefits will be different. That's because normal retirement age is gradually increasing to age 67. Table 5.2 shows the current benefit as a percentage of PIA that's payable at certain ages.

As you can see, you don't have to wait until normal retirement age to begin receiving benefits; you can begin receiving early retirement benefits at age 62. Depending on your retirement age, the benefit amount may be equal to, less than, or greater than the AIME. If you choose to retire early at 62, for example, the amount is reduced by approximately 0.56% for each month before normal retirement age. However, receiving early retirement benefits can be advantageous; although you'll receive a reduced benefit if you retire early, you'll receive benefits for a longer period than someone who retires at full retirement age.

Rick's Tip

You can also choose to delay receiving retirement benefits past normal retirement age. If you delay retirement, the Social Security benefit you eventually receive will be higher. That's because you'll receive a delayed retirement credit for each month you delay receiving retirement benefits, up to age 70. The amount of this credit varies, depending on your year of birth. If you elect to delay receiving benefits beyond the normal retirement age, but prior to age 70, the benefits are increased by 8% a year up to 140% of the normal benefit.

Table 5.2 - Benefit, as a percentage of Primary Insurance Amount (PIA), payable at ages 62-67 and age 70

Year of birth	Normal Retirement Age (NRA)	Credit for each year of delayed retirement after NRA (percent)	Benefit, as a percentage of PIA, beginning at age—						
			62	63	64	65	66	67	70
1924	65	3	80	86 2/3	93 1/3	100	103	106	115
1925-26	65	3½	80	86 2/3	93 1/3	100	103 1/2	107	117 1/2
1927-28	65	4	80	86 2/3	93 1/3	100	104	108	120
1929-30	65	4½	80	86 2/3	93 1/3	100	104 1/2	109	122 1/2
1931-32	65	5	80	86 2/3	93 1/3	100	105	110	125
1933-34	65	5½	80	86 2/3	93 1/3	100	105 1/2	111	127 1/2
1935-36	65	6	80	86 2/3	93 1/3	100	106	112	130
1937	65	6½	80	86 2/3	93 1/3	100	106 1/2	113	132 1/2
1938	65, 2 mo.	6½	79 1/6	85 5/9	92 2/9	98 8/9	105 5/12	111 11/12	131 5/12
1939	65, 4 mo.	7	78 1/3	84 4/9	91 1/9	97 7/9	104 2/3	111 2/3	132 2/3
1940	65, 6 mo.	7	77½	83 1/3	90	96 2/3	103 1/2	110 1/2	131 1/2
1941	65, 8 mo.	7½	76 2/3	82 2/9	88 8/9	95 5/9	102 1/2	110	132 1/2
1942	65, 10 mo.	7½	75 5/6	81 1/9	87 7/9	94 4/9	101 ¼	108 ¾	131 1/4
1943-54	66	8	75	80	86 2/3	93 1/3	100	108	132
1955	66, 2 mo.	8	74 1/6	79 1/6	85 5/9	92 2/9	98 8/9	106 2/3	130 2/3

1956	66, 4 mo.	8	73 1/3	78 1/3	84 4/9	91 1/9	97 7/9	105 1/3	129 1/3
1957	66, 6 mo.	8	72 ½	77 ½	83 1/3	90	96 2/3	104	128
1958	66, 8 mo.	8	71 2/3	76 2/3	82 2/9	88 8/9	95 5/9	102 2/3	126 2/3
1959	66, 10 mo.	8	70 5/6	75 5/6	81 1/9	87 7/9	94 4/9	101 1/3	125 1/3
1960 and later	67	8	70	75	80	86 2/3	93 1/3	100	124

Note: Persons born on January 1 of any year should refer to the previous year of birth.

Family Benefits

As I mentioned at the beginning of this section, family members are entitled to a portion of a worker's benefits, under these specific circumstances:

- A retired worker's spouse may elect to receive the greater of one-half of the worker's benefit or his own benefit. It doesn't matter if the primary worker is still working and hasn't begun to draw benefits—the spouse may draw at his eligible age.

- A divorced spouse who was married for ten years or more to an insured worker and who hasn't remarried may draw under the same rules as a married spouse. This doesn't impact the benefits available to the insured worker. As a matter of fact, the insured worker could have several divorced spouses drawing upon his or her benefit, and could also be currently married to a spouse drawing benefits.

- The minor children and spouse caring for minor children of a retired worker may be eligible for benefits. For those of you who became parents when you were older, as I did, your children under the age of 18 (or 19, if not graduated from high school) will receive a check equal to one-half of your benefit. The same goes for your spouse if she is caring for a minor under age 16. The total payable to a family is limited by a family maximum benefit calculation.

- Finally, if an insured worker passes on, his family is entitled to certain benefits. Children under age 18 (or 19, if not graduated from high school) receive a benefit, as does a spouse caring for a minor child under age 16. The amount is subject to family maximums and is dependent upon the worker's AIME. A surviving spouse may elect to draw a widow's benefit at age 60, whether or not she was married to the worker at his time of death.

Rodgers' Recommendations for Understanding How Social Security Benefits are Calculated

- You're eligible to receive Social Security benefits if you've been employed and subject to Social Security taxes for at least 40 quarters; you may earn a maximum of four credits in one year, and credits are based on your total wages (and/or self-employment income) during the year.

- The Social Security administration computes your benefit by indexing all of your earnings over your working life against general wage levels.

- Those born before 1938 may begin receiving full Social Security benefits at age 65; for anyone born after that date, the age at which they may receive benefits is gradually increasing to 67.

- Family members may be eligible to receive a portion of a worker's benefit if the members meet certain conditions.

WHEN TO BEGIN TAKING BENEFITS

When should I start drawing my Social Security benefits? I'm asked this question more often than any other by my clients who are retiring before Social Security's normal retirement age. They all want to know if they should begin receiving benefits early with a smaller monthly amount, or wait for a larger monthly payment later they may not receive as long. In answering this question for yourself, you should take the following factors into consideration.

You could consider *drawing Social Security benefits early* if:

- The financial challenges facing Social Security in the future, which I discuss in more detail below, are well known. While it's unlikely changes to benefits would be made to those who are already retired, it could happen—especially to those who have done a good job of preparing for retirement and have adequate retirement income from other sources. You may delay drawing benefits only to find out the amount you were expecting to receive has been changed. In the meantime, you'll have been using your own savings to live on.

- Social Security is largely based on life expectancy. If your family health history suggests your retirement is likely to be shorter, then it may be wise to start drawing benefits when you can.

- Drawing Social Security early allows you to preserve you own savings longer. You'll need income from somewhere if you're retired at age 62. You can keep your own savings invested and growing longer by using your Social Security benefits to meet your living expenses.

You should consider *drawing Social Security benefits later* if:

- The first consideration you should take into account is whether you'll be continuing to work and have earned income between age 62 and normal retirement age. Social Security benefits are penalized if you make over a certain amount of income. It wouldn't be wise to draw reduced benefits only to have them penalized.

- The Social Security administration states if you live to the average life expectancy for your age, you'll receive about the same amount in lifetime benefits no matter when you start drawing benefits. In general, then, if you come from a family with longer life expectancies, you should come out ahead by delaying your benefits until normal retirement age.

- Your spouse may be eligible for a benefit based on your work record. If you die before your spouse, he may be eligible for a survivor benefit based on your work record, particularly if you've earned more than your spouse over your lifetime. In this case, you may want to delay starting your benefits in order to provide your spouse with a higher amount.

Buyer's Remorse on Your Benefits

No matter how much thought and research you put into when to begin drawing your Social Security benefits, there's always the possibility you'll have buyer's remorse after you start. Believe it or not, the Social Security administration permits you to stop drawing your benefits and then restart them later at the higher current rate. But you probably won't be surprised when I tell you there's a bit of a catch: you must repay all of the benefits you've received to that point. However, you won't owe any interest, and there will be no adjustment for inflation.

To accomplish this, you must file Social Security Form 521—Request for Withdrawal of Application. You can download the form at the Social Security website, www.ssa.gov. Social Security will calculate the amount you've been paid and request a check from you. Once you've paid back the benefits, you can apply again for benefits and start drawing at the higher rate.

Rick's Tip

If you've been paying tax on your benefits all those years, you may even be able to recover the taxes. You'll need to pick up a copy of the IRS publication 915, which has instructions and worksheets that guide you through the process.

The reasons some people may want to stop and restart their benefits are pretty clear. If you started drawing benefits in your early 60s and are now getting a check for $1,000 per month, you may be able to stop that benefit and restart with $1,500 per month. A little math can help you determine how many years it will take to come out ahead. On the other hand, you obviously need to live long enough to come out ahead. If you were to die in an accident the month after you changed over, your heirs would be out all of the benefits you paid back.

I recommend you be in good health with a good family history of long life expectancies before considering this strategy. The last point to consider is changes to the Social Security system may reduce your benefits in the future. It seems highly unlikely they would change benefits for existing retirees, but it is a possibility. We all know Social Security is on shaky financial footing.

Rodgers' Recommendations for When to Begin Taking Social Security Benefits

You may want to consider drawing Social Security benefits early if you believe the financial challenges currently facing the system will adversely affect your benefits, you're unsure about the length of your life expectancy, or you'd like to preserve your personal retirement savings.

You could consider drawing Social Security benefits later if you'll be continuing to work and have earned income between age 62 and normal retirement age, you come from a family with longer life expectancies, or you believe your spouse may outlive you and you want to provide him or her with a higher amount of your benefit.

If you start taking your Social Security benefit and later wish you hadn't, you can stop drawing your benefits and then restart them later at the higher current rate—but you must repay all of the benefits you've received to that point.

THE TAX ON YOUR BENEFITS—AND HOW TO REDUCE IT

Originally, the benefits received by retired workers weren't taxed as income because, the government reasoned, the money had already been subject to income tax. Once the Social Security system started having solvency issues (I talk about these problems in more detail in the next section), major legislation was passed in 1984 that was designed to address its impending insolvency. The legislation stipulated that the portion of Social Security contributions paid by the employer had not in fact, been taxed, so this portion of the benefit began being taxed for retired workers with incomes over $25,000 filing as single, or with combined incomes over $32,000 (if married filing jointly).

The portion of the benefits potentially subject to tax was 50%, because this was considered the employer's contribution (it didn't matter if you were a self-employed worker and had been paying the entire tax all along). In 1994, the portion of benefits potentially subject to tax was increased to 85%.

Rick's Tip

Keep in mind the amount of taxes a worker pays into the Social Security system isn't deductible from his or her federal income tax return—unlike state and local income taxes, which are deductible.

Three Steps to Determining Your Social Security Taxation

You can follow these three steps to determine the amount of your own benefit that's subject to tax.

Calculate Your Total Income

This includes nearly everything—interest and dividend income, including tax-free municipal bond income; taxable pensions; other investment income; wages; net income from rental properties; farm income; and IRA distributions. What you can exclude is interest income from U.S. savings bonds; excludable foreign-earned income; and tax-free distributions from a Roth IRA. Don't include your Social Security income at this point.

Calculate Your Allowable Deductions

The government does allow some deductions from your total income. The first items would be any allowable income losses—capital gains (up to $3,000); losses from rental properties; business losses; farm income losses (you would actually include these losses as part of the first step, when you calculate your total income). The other allowable losses appear at the bottom of page one on IRS form 1040. On the 2008 form 1040, these are the items in lines 23 through 35 and include contributions to an IRA or SEP IRA; Health Savings Account deductions; tuition and fees; self-employed health insurance; etc.

Determine Your Filing Status and Corresponding Benefits Tax

Your next move should be to figure out which of the filing status categories you fit into, which will then clue you in about your corresponding tax. You can refer to the table below to find out both.

Table 5.3 - Filing Status Categories		
If your income plus half of your benefits exceeds...	...50% of your Social Security benefits will be taxed.	...85% of your Social Security benefits will be taxed.
$25,000 if single, head of household, or qualifying widow(er)	X	
$32,000 if married, filing jointly	X	
$34,000 if single, head of household or qualifying widow(er)		X
$44,000 if married, filing jointly		X

Strategies to Reduce the Tax on Your Benefits

Knowing how Social Security benefits are taxed helps when devising strategies to minimize the taxation of those benefits. First, I'll delve into more detail about the two main strategies: changing investment income and planning IRA distributions.

Two Strategies for Reducing Your Social Security Benefits Tax

Changing Investment Income

Most people structure their investments to produce income in retirement, since they're no longer working and now rely on their investment income to meet daily living expenses. It makes sense, then, to attempt to maximize the yield on their investments to produce the highest income. Investments like certificates of deposit (CDs), government and/or corporate bonds, preferred stocks, and income mutual funds are typically used as the investments of choice.

This approach may make investment sense, but it doesn't make tax sense when drawing Social Security benefits. All of the income produced by these investment vehicles will be used to make more of your benefits taxable. Income from municipal bonds and tax-free mutual funds are used to determine the taxable amount of your benefit, even though the interest from these investments is not taxable.

For example, if you had $500,000 invested in income producing investments with an overall yield of 5%, the investment portfolio would be producing $25,000 of income that would be used in the calculation for taxing your benefits. If you were a single filer, you'd already be at the first base level of taxation.

Instead of investing all of the money in income investments, you could invest $200,000 in a 10-year income annuity yielding 5%. The income annuity would make 120 monthly payments totaling $25,000 per year for 10 years. The remaining $300,000 could be invested in a growth vehicle like a tax-managed growth mutual fund or a variable annuity. Either one of these investments would produce little or no taxable income. If the growth investment averaged 5% per year, it would be worth $500,000 at the end of 10 years. The income annuity would be depleted to zero during the same time. You would have maintained your principal and income stream.

The really exciting result of this strategy would be what happens to the taxation of your Social Security benefits. The $25,000 you would receive as income wouldn't all be taxed as income, because $20,000 per year would be considered a return of your principal. Only $5,000 would be taxed as income, and only $5,000 would be used to determine the taxability of your benefits. At the end of the 10 years, you'd split up your growth investment and do the same thing for another period of time.

Rick's Tip

You could achieve a similar result by investing in growth oriented mutual funds and taking systematic withdrawals. Part of each withdrawal would be considered a return of principal, and the rest will be taxed as earnings. Note, however, this would be riskier than using an immediate annuity, because mutual funds aren't guaranteed. The tax on the investment earnings would be lower, because once you had held the fund for one year, the distributions would be considered long-term capital gains, which currently have a lower rate of tax than annuity income.

Planning IRA Distributions

Again, after you reach age 70½, you must begin taking minimum distributions from your IRA account. Those distributions are considered income to be used in determining the taxability of your Social Security benefits.

Most people will use the Uniform Lifetime Table we previously discussed to determine their minimum IRA distribution. It's the most commonly used of three life-expectancy charts that help retirement account holders figure mandatory distributions. (The other tables are for beneficiaries of retirement funds and account holders who have much younger spouses.) If you have an IRA balance of $100,000 at the end of the year before your 70½ birthday, you'll need to withdrawal $3,650 according to the Uniform Lifetime Table. Each year, the withdrawals should increase as you get older and the account continues to grow, because you're only taking out the minimum amount. If your income falls near the base amounts, these minimum distributions could prove costly in terms of the taxation of your Social Security benefits.

Therefore a little advance planning could go a long way toward reducing tax on your benefits. One good plan for combating this taxation is to consider a Roth conversion of the type we talked about earlier in the book. You could avoid minimum distributions altogether by converting your IRA to a Roth IRA all in one year. This would result in a large tax bill the year of the conversion, but you may avoid a lot of additional tax on your benefits in future years.

Another plan is to accelerate withdrawals into a single year. Until you reach age 70½ and have to take minimum distributions, you have a lot of flexibility over IRA distributions. If you need to take $1,000 per month from your IRA for retirement income, you may want to take the $12,000 you need for next year in December of this year. This would accelerate the taxable income into every other year, potentially leaving you with a year of very little tax on Social Security benefits.

Of course, these strategies require a lot of tax planning and projections. You should work with a skilled tax planner if you're uncomfortable running these projections on your own. There are a few additional short cuts you can take to reduce the tax on your Social Security benefits:

- Make deductible IRA contributions if you have wages and are under age 70½. If you have self-employment income, make SEP or SIMPLE contributions to reduce your income.

- Use tax-managed mutual funds or passively managed funds that are more tax-efficient in your taxable accounts. Actively managed mutual funds that aren't specifically tax managed must distribute realized capital gains at the end of the year. The distributions are included as income in the calculation and negate your efforts to minimize the tax on your benefits.

- Harvest unrealized losses at year end. Remember, you can take a maximum net loss from investments of $3,000 on your tax return. This loss can also be used in the benefit calculation to reduce income.

Rodgers' Recommendations for Reducing Tax on Social Security Benefits

- To figure out the taxes on your Social Security benefit, you must do the following three things: calculate your total income, calculate your allowable deductions, and determine your filing status.

- To reduce that tax, you can alter both your investment income and your IRA distributions in a tax-advantaged way.

SOCIAL SECURITY REFORM

The Social Security system has been running surpluses since the 1980s, when we had the last major overhaul of the system. The surpluses are being accounted for in a trust that totaled $2.048 billion at the end of 2006, according to the 2007 Old Age Survivor and Disability Insurance (OASDI) Trustees Report. However, the first of 75 million baby boomers became eligible for early Social Security benefits at the beginning of 2008. As more people start drawing benefits, the system will cease to generate a surplus and will begin to draw on the trust fund assets. The following is the conclusion of the trustees from their 2007 report:

> *Annual cost will begin to exceed tax income in 2017 for the combined OASDI Trust Funds, which are projected to become exhausted and thus unable to pay scheduled benefits in full on a timely basis in 2041 under the long-range intermediate assumptions. For the trust funds to remain solvent throughout the 75-year projection period, the combined payroll tax rate could be increased during the period in a manner equivalent to an immediate and permanent increase of 1.95 percentage points, benefits could be reduced during the period in a manner equivalent to an immediate and permanent reduction of 13.0 percent, general revenue transfers equivalent to $4.7 trillion in present value could be made during the period, or some combination of approaches could be adopted. Significantly larger changes would be required to maintain solvency beyond 75 years.*

Obviously, Social Security must be fixed. Because Social Security operates almost entirely as a pay-as-you-go system, it's been highly sensitive to the dramatic demographic changes over the last several decades. In addition to the first of the baby boomers now turning 62, today's life expectancy of a couple retiring at age 62 is 30 years. The current system has only a little over three workers to each retiree today, and that ratio will fall to two workers per retiree in the near future. Together, this falling ratio of workers to beneficiaries will push the system toward insolvency.

The sooner we act, the better. Every year we wait to address this problem, the cost of fixing it grows. The current system will start spending more money than it collects in 2017. It will take $6 trillion to repay the Social Security Trust Fund through 2041. Once this happens, benefits will need to be cut 26%, or the government will need to come up with another $25 trillion to cover promised benefits through 2077. While Social Security reform inevitably involves difficult choices, there's no future date at which those choices will be any less difficult than they are today.

Rick's Tip

Social Security taxes ought to be used for Social Security. Until 2017, workers will pay more into Social Security than is needed to pay current benefits. Because the federal government can't save this surplus—the so-called "trust fund" is really a deficit—a reflection of a liability, not an asset.

Unrealistic Reform Options

While it's clear Social Security can't continue to distribute future benefits at its current rate, the question of what to do about it remains to be answered. Fix-it plans that have recently been proposed are:

Plan One: Immediately reduce benefits by 13%
Plan Two: Raise payroll taxes by 3.5% from the current 12.4%

It's pointless to compare the benefits or taxes related to the various reform proposals against benefit and tax levels of the current system, when the promises of the current system aren't fundable under existing scheduled tax rates. No matter which option the country chooses, there will be no free lunch—no one will get something for nothing. What we get out of Social Security is a function of what we put into it, so it follows putting more taxes into the system will make workers worse off and retirees better off; putting less taxes into Social Security will do the opposite. We can't pretend these choices and trade-offs don't exist. So let's talk now about those consequences as they relate to each option.

Consequences of Current Fix-It Plans

If Social Security benefits aren't immediately reduced by 13% (a very unpopular decision), then they'd have to be cut by 26% in 2041, growing to over 32% in 2079. According to a recent study[2], these cuts would lead to a doubling of the poverty rate among seniors.

Congress could also opt to increase taxes in order to maintain promised benefit levels. They could raise payroll taxes now from the current 12.4% to 15.9%[3] (again, a very unpopular decision). Failing to raise taxes now would require an eventual 50% increase in taxes by 2041, which would have a dramatic impact on our economy. Social Security is already the largest and most regressive federal tax paid by two-thirds of working families, 80% of whom already pay more in payroll taxes than they do in federal income taxes. It's a head tax on employment that's paid on the first dollar of wages earned, whether or not the company is profitable.

---

2   Andrew Biggs. "The Distributional Consequences of a 'No-Action' Scenario," Social Security Administration, Policy Brief no. 2004-01, http://www.ssa.gov/policy/docs/policybriefs/pb2004-01.html#mn6 (2004).

3   Secretary of the Treasury John W. Snow, Prepared Remarks: The Wilmington Club, http://www.treasury.gov/press/releases/js2333.htm (March 24, 2005).

Another important consideration: when Social Security taxes go up in the United States, they don't go up in China. The trade implications of an increase in taxes would be immense. It's an underappreciated fact that increases in payroll taxes, particularly increases in the wage cap, will lead to dramatic reductions in employment.

Let's assume, then, we all agree: the current fix-it plans aren't viable options. Implementing one of them would result in either draconian benefit cuts, huge tax increases, or some combination of both. Yet obstruction and demagoging of reform will, by default, result in the inevitable implementation of one of these plans.

Realistic Reform Criteria

A more realistic approach to fixing the Social Security system would be to make changes to the system based on the following three criteria:

1. **Protect the benefits of those already in or near retirement.** Most workers born prior to 1950 don't have enough time to prepare their finances to adjust for potential Social Security reforms.

2. **Place the burden of reform on higher wage workers while protecting middle and low income workers.** Every future retiree under any reform plan that indexes benefits based on prices will be guaranteed a benefit in real dollars that's at least equal to the benefits received by today's retirees. The concept of "progressive indexing" promises lower and middle income workers substantially more than current retirees—while giving the highest wage workers an amount equal to today's retirees. Considering the size of the shortfall we face, this seems fair.

3. **Personal savings accounts ought to be a part of Social Security reform.** Prudence calls for directing surplus Social Security

taxes into personal accounts that are owned by, managed by, and protected for the American workers. This would prevent the federal government from raiding the Social Security trust fund like it does now in order to report lower budget deficits. Opponents of privatization claim diverting $134 billion of surplus payroll taxes into personal retirement accounts is "robbing Social Security." Yet using those same resources to fund other government programs and replacing the funds with IOUs is "protecting Social Security." This doesn't make any sense.

Safe investments and years of compounding would provide workers with real ownership of their retirements, real choices, and peace of mind the current system doesn't offer. Moreover, most young people don't believe Social Security will be there when they're ready to retire. Privatization would help restore their faith in the system.

Rodgers' Recommendations for Reforming Social Security

- Neither of the two primary ideas for fixing Social Security that are currently on the federal government's table—reducing benefits or raising payroll taxes—are viable options for truly fixing the program.

- The key to real reform is privatizing Social Security by creating personal retirement accounts in which all workers could save a portion of their payroll taxes.

- Any reform plan chosen should aim to protect the benefits of those who are near to retirement or already retired, and the burden of reform should fall to higher wage earners in order to protect middle and lower wage earners.

***

By this point, we've covered nearly all of the bases involved in the game of retirement planning. There's just one more important topic I want to discuss—estate planning—before the book wraps up. Let's move on to the final chapter, where I tell you how to plan your estate in a manner that keeps the IRS at bay.

Chapter Six

Keep the IRS Out of Your Estate

FIVE REASONS TO REEXAMINE YOUR ESTATE PLAN

In a recent survey of affluent investors, 80% of respondents said they hadn't updated, reviewed, or had a conversation in regard to their estate plan in the last five years. What this likely means is that all of those respondents' estate plans have become outdated through circumstances such as changes in their family situations (marriage, new grandchildren, etc.), net worth additions or subtractions, or business and/or partnership changes.

There are many important reasons to periodically reexamine your estate plan and all of the documents related to it. Below are my top five.

1. **Your state has plans for your estate.** Everyone has an estate plan whether they know it or not: it's called, "by default!" That is, if you die without a will, your state has backup laws in place that dictate the disposition of your assets after your death. This means that if you die without a will, the state decides who receives your

assets—and there's no guarantee that the state will make the same decisions that you would have made.

If you don't have an updated will, don't feel badly about it, because you're not alone. According to a recent survey by legal web site FindLaw.com, 55% of Americans don't have a will, and 67% don't have a living will to express their wishes about end-of-life medical care. What's more, those who have a will often forget to update it.

2. **You can safeguard your estate even if you become incapacitated.** Should you become unable to make financial decisions, an estate plan allows you to designate someone to act on your behalf regarding your estate. You can also designate someone to be your surrogate to make decisions regarding your health and well-being.

3. **Estate planning helps with difficult end-of-life decisions.** Putting your wishes in writing relieves your family of the burden of making end-of-life decisions—decisions that may have profound emotional and financial consequences for them.

4. **Estate planning minimizes taxes.** You can maximize the amount of your estate that goes to heirs and minimize the amount that goes to the IRS.

5. **You can support your favorite charities.** If you have a favorite charity or cause, a gift from your estate can be an easy way to make a significant financial contribution.

Rodgers' Recommendations for Reexamining Your Estate Plan

- Keep your estate plan up-to-date. This ensures the disposition of your assets at death follow your wishes and not the rules of your state.

- Estate planning minimizes taxes and may maximize the amount that goes to your heirs.

- An estate plan and health care directive help your family carry out your wishes while minimizing conflict.

ESTATE TAX OVERVIEW

When it comes to your estate, there are two main types of tax you need to worry about: the federal estate tax and the federal gift tax.

Federal Estate Tax

As I mentioned earlier in the book, EGTRRA in 2001 changed the rules on the federal estate tax significantly. Unfortunately, the rules revert back to the way they were in 2001, which makes estate planning very difficult in the present. Essentially, a lot depends on when you're going to pass away.

Basically, we all have a lifetime exclusion from estate taxes we can use while we're living to shelter gifts or upon our death to shelter our estate. But the amount of that exclusion, as well as the tax on estates over the amount of the exclusion, vary each year until 2011. Table 6.1 includes year-to-year details.

Table 6.1 - Federal Estate Tax Exclusions		
Year	Amount of estate excluded from estate tax	Tax on estate amounts over the excluded amount
2008	$2 million	45%
2009	$3.5 million	45%
2010	Unlimited (the estate tax is repealed for this year!)	N/A
2011	$1 million	55%

Federal Gift Tax

One of the most common ways retirees attempt to skirt estate taxes is to give portions of their estates away as gifts before they die (I explain more details about gifting strategies in the next section). But this approach isn't without its own tax rules, otherwise known as the federal gift tax. This tax is paid by the donor on gifts that exceed $13,000 to any one recipient. You can use your lifetime exclusion to shelter gifts up to $1 million. However, when you're making gifts over $13,000 to one person, you're using up your lifetime exclusion, which could mean your estate will pay a lot more taxes when it's settled.

The gift tax and estate tax are similar and are taxed on the same scale, with one important difference: the gift tax is pre-tax, and the estate tax is after-tax. You don't include the gift taxes when figuring the value of a gift. The funds used to pay estate taxes are themselves subject to the tax. Therefore, a taxable gift is more favorable than having an asset taxed at death, because the funds used to pay gift taxes escape taxation.

Rodgers' Recommendations for Understanding Estate Taxes

- The two main types of estate taxes are the federal estate tax and the federal gift tax.

- A portion of your estate may be excluded from the federal estate tax, but the amount of the exclusion varies from year to year.

- You can shield part of your estate from taxes by giving it away before you die, but the maximum amount you can give tax-free is $13,000 per person, per year, or $1 million total over your lifetime.

GIFTING STRATEGIES FOR AVOIDING ESTATE TAXES

As I mentioned earlier, a sure-fire way to avoid paying tax on your estate is to give your money away as gifts while you're still living. Several gifting strategies exist that can help you accomplish this.

Annual Gift Tax Exclusion

One of the simplest estate planning strategies is to take advantage of the annual gift exclusion, which, remember, is currently $13,000 in 2009. If, for example, a husband and wife gave $13,000 to each of their three children every year, that would be $26,000 per child, times three, for a total of $78,000 given gift tax-free every year. Any grandchildren could also be given the same amount. A couple with a large estate who have several children and grandchildren could make sizable gifts every year to help keep their estate from getting too large.

529 College Savings Plan

Helping your grandchildren save for college by contributing to 529 College Savings Plans for them is an excellent way to give tax-free gifts from your estate. A 529 plan is a tax-advantaged investment account designed to encourage saving for the future higher education expenses of a designated beneficiary. Federal law allows you to contribute to each 529 account with a different beneficiary up to five times the annual gift tax exclusion amount in one year. 529 plans allow the earnings to grow tax-deferred, and distributions for the beneficiary's college costs are exempt from tax. Two of my clients, Bill and Audrey Jennings, took great advantage of this strategy, as demonstrated by the following case study.

Case Study: Bill and Audrey Jennings, retirees

Bill and Audrey Jennings had four adult children and seven grandchildren. Their estate was valued at a little over $5 million, and they wanted to start an annual gifting program. They decided they wanted to primarily gift to the grandchildren, because they were leaving the estate to their children. All of the grandchildren were minors, and the Jennings were concerned about how the money would be used once the grandchildren turned 21 and gained access to the funds.

The Jennings decided to gift their money into 529 College Savings Plans. While their contributions weren't deductible from their federal income tax return, as Pennsylvania residents, they could take a state income tax deduction for all or part of their contribution.

Rick's Tip

Many other states besides Pennsylvania provide an income tax deduction for residents who contribute to 529 College Savings Plans.

Because Bill and Audrey could each make gifts as individuals (rather than as a couple), their total contribution to each grandchild could be ten times the annual gift tax exclusion amount, or $130,000 to each grandchild. A gift tax return would need to be filed to use this provision. If they took advantage of the accelerated gift provision, any further gifts made to the same grandchild during the five-year period may be subject to gift taxes.

Another advantage from the Jennings' perspective was they, as donors, maintained control of the accounts. With few exceptions, the named beneficiary to a 529 plan has no rights to the funds. Most plans even allow donors to reclaim the funds for themselves any time they want.

Rick's Tip

If you reclaim the funds you've given to a 529 plan, keep in mind the earnings will be subject to income tax and a 10% penalty tax.

If you decide to go with a 529 strategy, remember a potential drawback is withdrawals from the account must be spent on eligible college expenses. Money spent for any other purpose will be subject to income tax plus an additional 10% federal tax penalty.

Unlimited Gift Tax Exclusion for Tuition

You can also make tax-free estate gifts for your grandkids' college expenses in another way: through the unlimited gift tax exclusion allowed for tuition you pay directly to a qualifying educational organization. It doesn't matter what your relationship is to the beneficiary to use this exclusion. The exception doesn't apply to expenses like books, dormitory fees, or room and board. You can also use this exclusion to pay health care providers directly for medical care for someone else, and payments for medical insurance also qualify for the unlimited gift tax exclusion. Note that using these exclusions doesn't have an impact on the $13,000 annual gift tax exclusion limit; you'd still be able to gift up to $13,000 per year to the same person.

Trusts

The biggest drawback to estate planning lies in the fact that to get assets out of your estate, you must give them away and/or give up control. In fact, one of the tests the IRS uses to determine if an asset should be included in your estate is whether or not you've retained any ownership interest. For example, putting money into a custodial account for a minor is a completed gift. However, if you name yourself as the custodian of the account until the minor turns age 21, you've retained control of the account. The value of the custodial account will be included in your estate.

Rick's Tip

The IRS is constantly looking to shoot down the use of trusts in estate planning. It's imperative you work with a competent estate planner to make sure you follow all the rules to the letter.

The primary reason we use trusts in estate planning is to give property away but not give up total control. Therefore, caution is advised when pursuing one of the trust strategies I describe below.

Grantor Trusts

The following example of my clients, Richard and Thelma Eastman, shows you how grantor trusts work.

Case Study: Richard and Thelma Eastman, retirees

Richard and Thelma Eastman had an estate valued at $4 million. Their wills left everything to the surviving spouse and then equally to their four children when the second spouse passed away. The problem with this arrangement was the surviving spouse would have had an estate of $4 million, half of which would've been subject to federal estate tax. Under this strategy, the IRS would help itself to $900,000 in estate taxes.

In the Eastmans' situation, we decided to separate their property equally and establish a separate grantor trust for Richard and Thelma, each funded with half the assets. The creation of these trusts had no income or estate tax implications. The trusts were revocable, so the income flowed through the trusts to the Eastman's tax return in the same way it did before the trusts were created.

The advantage of this strategy would come when one of the spouses passed away. Richard's trust would become irrevocable upon his death, and the assets in the trust would be exposed to tax. However, because Richard had a $2 million exclusion that hadn't been used for gifting, there would be no estate tax on the trust assets, since they totaled only $2 million. The provision of his trust stated the assets would belong to his children but would be retained in the trust as long as Thelma was living. She'd be entitled to all of the income from the trust. Provided all of the income was distributed to her, there would be no income tax due on the trust. When Thelma died, the assets would be released from Richard's trust and passed to the children. Thelma's trust wouldn't be used, because Richard had passed away first. Her assets would go directly to the children. Overall, the strategy saved the children $900,000 of estate taxes.

A variation of the strategy employed by the Eastmans can be used for purposes other than to save estate taxes, as you can see in the case of my clients, Roy and Mary Ellen Carter.

Case Study: Roy and Mary Ellen Carter, retirees

Roy and Mary Ellen Carter married late in life, after both of them lost their first spouses. Each had children from their earlier marriages and wanted to make sure their individual assets were passed to their own children. They had a total estate of $2 million, so there was no concern about federal estate taxes. However, they also recognized their responsibility to each other in the marriage and wanted to make sure the survivor had enough assets to maintain his or her lifestyle.

Roy and Mary Ellen both established a revocable grantor trust to hold the assets they both brought to the marriage. When one of them died, their trust would convert to an irrevocable trust for the benefit of their children. The surviving spouse would be able to take all of the income from the trust during the rest of his or her lifetime. Upon the second spouse's death, the assets in the trust would be passed on to the children.

Insurance Trusts

Insurance is commonly misused in estate planning. People often implement an insurance strategy because insurance proceeds bypass probate costs and go directly to the beneficiary, and the death benefit itself is generally not subject to estate taxes. However, the value of the death benefit may be included in the value of the estate, making other assets subject to estate tax. This problem is created when the insured and the policy owner are the same person. The policy owner has ownership rights, and therefore the IRS deems the policy value will be included in the estate.

Another reason an insurance strategy is often implemented in estate planning is to create liquidity in order to pay the estate tax. Liquidity is frequently needed when a significant portion of the estate is a closely held business or a valuable real estate holding, such as a family farm. We also come across the need to provide liquidity when a significant asset is a tax-deferred retirement account. In the story you read about the Richardsons in the introduction to this book, the heirs were forced to take money out of Frank's retirement account to pay the estate taxes, because the only other asset in the estate was the business ownership that couldn't be easily sold. The distribution itself was subject to income taxes, which started a tax spiral that ended up consuming over 80% of Frank's retirement account.

To avoid these situations, an insurance trust can be created to both generate liquidity and remove the policy from the estate. Consider the following case study about my clients, Jay and Evelyn Roberts.

Case Study: Jay and Evelyn Roberts, retirees

The estate of Jay and Evelyn Roberts had passed the $5 million mark. The estate consisted of a farm valued at $1½ million, retirement accounts of $1 million, and $2½ million in various bank and investment accounts. They'd separated their assets equally and opted to put a credit shelter provision in their will rather than establish grantor trusts while they were alive. In the event of one spouse's death, the assets in the deceased's name would go into an irrevocable trust and be held for the children. The income would pass to the surviving spouse while he or she was alive. Using the will instead of setting up the grantor trusts while they were both living accomplished the goal of preserving each of their lifetime credits.

The Roberts' total estate of $5 million would be left with only $1 million taxable after the credit shelter trusts. The heirs would have a tax bill of $450,000. There were sufficient liquid assets to pay the bill, so nothing needed to be done to provide liquidity. They could have started an aggressive gifting strategy to their children and grandchildren to reduce the taxable portion of the estate. They also could have explored select charities to support that would exempt the charitable portion from estate taxes.

Instead, a life insurance agent talked them into buying a $1 million policy on Evelyn's life to provide cash to pay the estate tax. What this agent accomplished was to inflate the estate by $1 million, which raised the estate tax bill to $900,000. The policy was owned by Evelyn, and she was also the insured, so their estate was ultimately valued at $6 million—and $2 million was taxed at 45%.

In the Roberts' case, they ultimately had plenty of liquid assets, so an insurance policy wasn't necessary for estate liquidity. After all, it didn't make a lot of sense for them to spend $80,000 per year for insurance premiums when they could have simply given the $80,000 outright to their heirs.

If the Roberts' had not had plenty of liquid assets, the proper way for them to have used insurance would have been to first establish an irrevocable life insurance trust (ILIT) that would own the policy and also serve as beneficiary. The Roberts would gift the premium payments to the trust. In this way, an ILIT becomes a great technique to use when the estate holds large amounts of illiquid assets. Typically, we'd use a second-to-die policy. The policy would be based on both Jay's and Evelyn's lives, but the death benefit wouldn't be paid until the last one passed away. (The proceeds are not needed to pay estate taxes until the second spouse dies in this situation.) Second-to-die insurance doesn't cost as much, because it's based on two lives instead of one.

Rick's Tip

The gifting limits must still be observed when using an insurance trust. The premium payments for Evelyn's policy were $80,000 per year. They have three children who would all be listed as equal beneficiaries under the trust. While both Jay and Evelyn were living, they could gift $24,000 to each child, for a total of $72,000 in tax-free gifts. This amount wouldn't quite cover the premiums required to support the policy. The Roberts would need to file a gift tax return each year, which would eat into their lifetime credit, or name the grandchildren as beneficiaries to increase the amount of tax-free gifts they could make each year.

Grantor Retained Annuity Trust (GRAT)

Grantor Retained Annuity Trusts (GRATs) represent yet another type of trust you may use to protect your estate from taxes, as my clients, Jerry and Sylvia Anderson, did.

Case Study: Jerry and Sylvia Anderson, retirees

Jerry and Sylvia Anderson had an estate valued at $3 million, which was comprised of their $500,000 home and $2½ million worth of securities. Each had sizable pension and Social Security incomes that provided all of the money they needed to maintain their lifestyle. When the Andersons both turned 70, they became concerned their estate would continue to grow beyond their ability to avoid estate taxes. They only had one child, so the most they could gift tax-free was $24,000 per year. The $2½ million investment account would earn far more than the amount they could gift.

The technique we chose to use was to maximize their lifetime gifting exclusion of $1 million. They could simply gift $2 million to their son (they could each give $1 million), which would reduce their estate and minimize the amount of future growth. We also wanted the technique to allow us to discount the present value of the gift in order to give larger sums of money.

The Andersons' strategy began by establishing an irrevocable trust for their son that paid income back to the couple over a period of time. We determined the trust would make distributions of 5% per year for a period of 10 years.

Rick's Tip

Note that the interest rate used isn't arbitrary; it's established by the Internal Revenue Code Section 7520 and changes monthly. The IRS recognizes that the value of the future income reduces the present value of the gift.

The Andersons were able to gift $2.4 million to the trust, but it counted only as a gift of $973,000. At the end of the 10 years, the balance remaining in the trust would go directly to their son. If the trust actually earned 8% over the 10 years, the son would receive $3.2 million at the end of the term. The Andersons could also gift back $24,000 per year of the payments using the annual tax-free exclusion, which would amount to another $240,000 passed tax-free to their son. In addition, the annual gifting would minimize the amount of growth that would accumulate in their own estate from the annuity payments. The Andersons would need to file a gift tax return claiming the present value of the trust and using it against their lifetime exclusions.

Be aware there's one big catch to the GRAT strategy: the IRS takes the position that the entire value of the trust must be added to the Andersons' estate if they die during the term of the GRAT.

Rodgers' Recommendations for Gifting Strategies to Avoid Estate Taxes

- You can achieve substantial estate tax savings by making use of the $13,000 annual gift tax exclusion.

- It's important to remember you're legally transferring your wealth to someone else. The tax savings is for your heirs, not you.

- Remember when making gifts of appreciated assets to people that they receive the asset at your cost for capital gains tax purposes. You should calculate whether the capital gains tax or the estate/inheritance tax will be less.

ESTATE PLANNING WITH A ROTH IRA

Earlier in this book, we talked a lot about how the Roth IRA is a great tool to use in your retirement savings plan. This extends to estate plans as well, since the Roth IRA can optimize estate plans for taxpayers with significant assets in retirement plans. If you count yourself among this group, a Roth IRA has the potential to provide a great source of wealth for your heirs.

Let's examine the advantages of a Roth IRA in an estate plan by taking a look at the choices of two different men, Dave Kline and Bob Costa.

Case Study: Dave Kline and Bob Costa, estate holders

Dave Kline had a $300,000 IRA he elected to convert to a Roth IRA. He determined his other retirement assets—including his pension, Social Security, and $500,000 in after-tax savings—would be sufficient to provide all of his income needs throughout his life expectancy. Dave's plan was to allow the Roth to accumulate without taking distributions and spend down his after-tax savings. He anticipated when the time came to settle his estate, his Roth IRA would represent the most significant asset in his estate and he'd have fewer assets in the after-tax account.

Bob Costa also had a $300,000 IRA he elected to retain to avoid paying a huge tax bill on a Roth conversion. Once Bob turned 70½, his IRA would begin to diminish as he took the annual required minimum distributions. Bob anticipated that when his estate was settled, the IRA would represent a smaller account because of the minimum distributions. A larger portion of his estate would be in his after-tax accounts. The after-tax assets most likely wouldn't be touched, because the IRA distributions should be sufficient to meet Bob's income needs.

Let's run some projections to quantify the advantages of Dave's conversion and determine how both Bob's and Dave's money will grow and be used throughout their lifetimes. We'll start by comparing the projected outcomes from these two situations.

We'll assume Dave begins converting his IRA at age 65 and completes the conversion over three years. We do this so Dave won't pay more than 25% tax in any year. We'll also assume the tax is paid out of the IRA as the account is converted. The value of the Roth after conversion is $225,000. Dave's Roth will grow to $1,050,000 by the time he passes away at age 85, assuming an 8% growth rate.

Bob leaves his IRA untouched until he has to start taking minimum distributions at age 70½. His first year distribution is $16,000, and we withhold 25% for taxes and reinvest the difference in his after-tax accounts, which grows at 6% after-tax. Each year, Bob takes the minimum IRA distribution, withholds the tax, and reinvests the amount in his after-tax account. When Bob passes away at age 85, his IRA has a remaining balance of $663,750. The minimum distributions have totaled a net amount of $344,500 and have grown to $508,250. The total of Bob's two accounts is $1,172,000.

At the end of both Dave's and Bob's life expectancies, the two estates contain roughly the same value of assets. In fact, Bob's estate is worth $120,000 more than Dave's, which would seem to indicate just holding the IRA would be the better option. However, simply comparing the total number of dollars available to each estate at the time of the owner's death isn't a complete analysis. To fully appreciate the merits of inheriting a Roth IRA, we need to extend the analysis into the next generation.

Measured in immediate purchasing power, the estate containing the Roth IRA has a big advantage over the estate comprised of the pre-tax IRA and after-tax investments. An after-tax dollar in your pocket will buy the same cup of coffee as the dollar in your pocket from a Roth IRA. But the balance remaining in the IRA still has to be taxed before those dollars can be spent. Applying the same 25% tax level to the $663,750 balance in Bob's IRA nets his heirs only $500,000. Dave's Roth now has roughly a $40,000 advantage over Bob's estate measured in immediate purchasing power.

If both sets of heirs were to liquidate the accounts and spend the money, the story would end here. However, when the heirs maintain the accounts and take only the minimum required distributions through their lifetime, the advantage of the Roth IRA conversion stands out even more.

Bob's 60-year-old child starts to take minimum distributions from the IRA, paying tax at the rate of 25% each year. The child's life expectancy ends at age 85, when the net distributions will have totaled $1.5 million. Combining this with the after-tax account brings the total value of Bob's estate to his heir to a little over $2 million.

Dave's 60-year-old child starts taking their minimum distribution from his Roth IRA. The same life expectancy applies to Dave's heir, so when the child reaches age 85, the distributions will have totaled $3.2 million—over 50% more than Bob's estate that maintained an IRA!

Throughout this book I've made the case for the Roth IRA and how it should be an integral part of your retirement plan. The level of control over your income taxes is significantly hampered without having a Roth account to draw on. As this section demonstrates, the power of the Roth doesn't end at life expectancy. The potential value Roth IRAs have in an estate is enormous. Making a significant Roth IRA conversion is usually very beneficial for both you and your heirs. I'd argue in favor of a Roth IRA conversion even if the conversion doesn't significantly impact your retirement income. When your child or grandchild is named as the beneficiary of a Roth IRA, and he elects to take only minimum distributions from the Roth, the Roth's value is substantially greater than the value of the same amount of after-tax funds.

Rick's Tip

The challenge of realizing the maximum wealth potential from an inherited Roth IRA will fall to your heirs. It's essential your beneficiaries understand the value is achieved over time, and the Roth IRA should be preserved in its tax-free environment as long as possible.

Rodgers' Recommendations for Estate Planning with a Roth IRA

- The Roth IRA in estate planning can be of even greater value to you than it is in your retirement income planning.

- Analysis of an IRA conversion to a Roth needs to be measured in immediate purchasing power instead of total dollars. Pre-tax dollars and after-tax dollars don't have the same purchasing power.

- Educate your heirs and beneficiaries about the value of taking distributions from the inherited Roth IRA over time. The total wealth generated for them could be measured in the millions!

BENEFICIARIES: KEY TO ANY SOLID ESTATE PLAN

For most people, filling in the names of beneficiaries for retirement assets and life insurance policies is an autopilot task. The primary beneficiary is a spouse; secondary is a child or children. Others simply leave the beneficiary designation blank, and few of us think about updating beneficiaries once they're designated. Yet designating and updating beneficiaries is key to estate planning, because it affects how your assets are dispersed after your death and the quality of life for your heirs.

When I have estate planning sessions with my clients, I often find the same questions crop up consistently. The following are seven of those very common questions, along with my answers for each.

1. **Why is it important to name beneficiaries?** When you designate a beneficiary for your 401(k), IRA, or life insurance policy, the money in those accounts becomes immediately available to the beneficiary upon your death. If you don't name a beneficiary, those assets will probably go into your estate. A probate court would then dispose of the assets in your estate according to your will. However, the probate process can take months, sometimes years—depriving your heirs of access to your assets until the estate is settled.

2. **Doesn't my will override everything else, including named beneficiaries?** On the contrary, if you have a named beneficiary, that designation overrides your will. That's why it's vitally important to keep beneficiaries updated for all of your assets.

3. **Am I required to name my spouse as my beneficiary?** It depends. Most insurance policies and IRAs don't require you to name your spouse as your primary beneficiary. However, most qualified plans require your spouse to sign a waiver if you choose not to name him or her as your primary beneficiary. If you live in a community property state, your spouse may have rights to the assets in your IRA regardless of whether or not he or she is named as primary beneficiary. Check with your estate planning advisor for more information.

4. **Are there any advantages to naming my spouse as the primary beneficiary of my retirement assets?** In general, your spouse has more flexibility than a non-spouse. For example, your spouse can roll over your retirement assets to a qualified plan or IRA in his or her own name, thereby delaying required minimum distributions until age 70½. Non-spouse beneficiaries, on the other hand, must either begin taking distributions soon after your death or deplete the account within about five years after you die.

5. **How many beneficiaries can I name?** Many people think they can name only two beneficiaries because two lines appear on most designation forms. But there's no limit to the number of primary or secondary beneficiaries you can name for any plan. If you run out or room on your beneficiary form, ask if you can attach a sheet of paper with additional designations.

6. **Can I name my minor children as beneficiaries?** Yes, but keep in mind that if they are minors when you die, someone will need to be named to manage the assets until the children reach the age of maturity. It's possible to set up a trust in your minor children's names and then designate the trust as beneficiary. However, creating and dealing with trusts can be complicated. Your estate planning advisor can help you make decisions about naming your minor children as beneficiaries.

7. **How often should I review my beneficiaries?** Whenever you experience a major life event—marriage, divorce, the birth or adoption of a child, or the death or disability of a loved one—it's a good idea to review your beneficiary designations.

Because talking about death is difficult, many families overlook some basics for helping loved ones cope more easily during a stressful time. Not knowing the location of your will or safe deposit key, for example, can cause unnecessary worries for family members.

In addition to creating an estate plan, take the time now to make the arrangements listed below, in order to help your family after your death.

Funeral or Memorial Service Plans

You can save your family members added grief and potential conflict by discussing your wishes with them and leaving precise written instructions regarding the following decisions:

- Burial or cremation
- Funeral or memorial service
- Open or closed casket
- Wake, viewing, or neither
- Place of burial
- Flowers or donations to a charity
- Music and readings for a service
- Specific information you'd like included in an obituary

Updated Records

Keep a current list of all of your assets and property. If your heirs are unaware of an insurance policy or investment you own, it could end up being awarded to the state if the rightful owner can't be identified. In addition, keep a file with your most recent account statements, and make sure the executor of your will knows where to find this file.

Important Documents

Store the important documents below in a safe place, and tell your heirs and your executor where they are and how to access them.

- Funeral plans
- Recent statements and beneficiary information for your retirement and/or pension plans
- Bank account information
- Will and any trust documents
- Deeds and title information for any property you own, including real estate and cars
- Location and contents of all safes and safe deposit boxes
- Information regarding any stocks, bonds, or mutual funds you own
- Living will
- Durable power of attorney
- Birth certificate and marriage license
- Military service records, if applicable
- Social Security number
- All auto, home, and life insurance policies
- Mortgage information
- Most recent tax return

Rodgers' Recommendations for Naming and Assisting Beneficiaries

- If you don't designate beneficiaries for your 401(k), IRA, and life insurance policies, the assets may be tied up in probate court for a long time.

- Review your beneficiary designations after a major life change.

- For qualified plans, you must name your spouse as primary beneficiary unless he or she gives written authorization for you to do otherwise.

- You may name as many beneficiaries as you wish.

- Keep a current list of all of your assets and property.

- Consider storing this information in a safe deposit box, fire-proof safe, or file cabinet, and make sure the appropriate parties have access or know where to find the key.

- Discuss funeral or memorial service arrangements with your family and leave written instructions.

✳✳✳

We've reached the end of our exploration of the most tax-efficient ways to structure your retirement savings plan. At several points throughout this book, you probably stopped to dream about what your days will be like when you finally retire. I hope you envisioned times when you felt relaxed, enjoyed family and friends, and engaged in activities you love. After working hard for many years, retirement should be one of the best stages of your life that's filled with all of these things and more.

Your retirement *should not* involve stress and anxiety about whether you've accumulated enough savings to support yourself in your golden years—and whether the IRS is going to deplete your savings through excessive taxation. The knowledge you've gained throughout the book will help you avoid this stress, since the tax-efficient plan you're going to implement based on your newfound knowledge will both help your retirement assets grow now, and steer the IRS away from taxing those assets later.

Above all, remember one thing: your Three-Legged Stool should be balanced among the three primary types of retirement savings plans—pre-tax, after-tax, and tax-free. Not only is it important to strike a balance when establishing and contributing to these accounts, you must also remain aware of the tax implications involved in withdrawing from the accounts when you retire. If all of this seems daunting, don't worry; there are good financial advisors out there who can help you connect the dots. Just use the tips I gave you to find one.

Here's wishing you and your family a wonderful retirement.

Appendix

How to Write a Personal Financial Plan

At several points throughout my book, *How To Stop The IRS From Stealing 75% Of Your Retirement,* I stress the importance of working with a knowledgeable financial advisor to build and execute your retirement plan. This doesn't mean, however, you can simply sit back and expect your advisor to act entirely on his or her own. Don't forget, you are still the most important person in the process; after all, it's your future!

One of best ways to achieve success with your financial advisor is to write a personal financial plan. From your professional life, you may be familiar with writing a business plan; the financial plan I'm talking about is like a business plan, except it's for investing. This plan should have two parts. First, it should clearly state the terms of communication you'll have with your advisor—how and when your advisor will keep you informed about the status of your investments. Second, it should outline your expectations for your investments themselves, defining your financial goals as well as the type of portfolio you'll build to achieve those goals.

While many investors get only generic recommendations from their advisors, writing a personal financial plan like the kind I've described is your chance to be specific. You'll never regret putting the way you want your account managed in writing. This way, if anything goes wrong, you and your advisor can always refer to your plan to get back on track.

PART ONE: ESTABLISH CLEAR ADVISOR-CLIENT COMMUNICATION

Your financial advisor may be doing a fantastic job of managing your retirement assets, but if the two of you aren't on the same communication page, you could ultimately end up dissatisfied. It's not enough to achieve good returns on your investments; your advisor must also do a good job of keeping you posted on the status of these returns (or lack thereof). Remember, though—while you should be able to expect a lot of things from a financial advisor, mind-reading isn't one of them. Sufficient communication means different things to different people, and it's up to you to define your version of good communication to your advisor so he has a clear understanding of your expectations.

Make the following three steps to clear client-advisor communication an official part of your personal financial plan. Don't just have a casual conversation about them with your advisor; put the terms you agree to down on the same paper that contains your expectations for your investments themselves (which we'll talk about in part two below). This way, both you and your advisor will take your communications commitments seriously.

Three Steps to Establishing Clear Client-Advisor Communication

1. **Establish a maximum timeframe within which your advisor will return your phone calls.** As with any business, your advisor will likely have many clients but should always do her best to make you feel you're the only one! This means returning your phone calls promptly, which is an immediate indication of responsiveness to your needs. In your plan, be specific about how long it will take for your advisor to get back to you; for example, instead of writing, "my calls will be returned promptly," specify, "my calls will be returned within two business days"—and hold your advisor to it! Never accept advisor excuses like, "I couldn't get back to you because I've been with other clients." Your business is too important for that.

2. **Set a schedule by which you will receive written updates on your portfolio.** Traditionally, financial services firms send their clients written updates on a quarterly basis. Expect no less than this from your advisor, and don't hesitate to ask for more frequent updates if this makes you feel more comfortable. With the convenience of the Internet and email, providing you with frequent updates is now easier than ever.

3. **Come to an agreement about how often you'll meet.** While you should feel free to call your advisor with your questions as they arise, you can also expect him to commit to regularly scheduled status meetings. These meetings ensure your advisor will set aside dedicated time to focus on you and your portfolio, and you should expect to hear a comprehensive, specific update on your portfolio's status each time you get together. Make sure you build in enough time to ask any additional questions you might have

after you hear the advisor's report, as well as to do any necessary portfolio readjustment.

PART TWO: CREATE A DETAILED INVESTMENT PLAN

Once you and your advisor have completed the communications portion of your personal financial plan, which will be based on your mutual understanding of how and when you will communicate, you can move on to part two: writing your investment plan.

This five-step exercise will help you as well as your advisor. Putting your investment thoughts in writing will encourage you to sort through any internal confusion or indecision you may have had about what exactly you want to have achieved upon retirement. It will also help your advisor to comprehend your current and long-term financial concerns and needs. Finally, it will assist both of you by setting forth guidelines for reviewing your goals and risk tolerance on a regular basis.

Rick's Tip

Regular portfolio reviews are a critical endeavor for any investor since, as we painfully experienced in the fall of 2008, circumstances in both the financial markets and/or your personal life can cause your goals to change over time.

Five Steps to Creating a Detailed Investment Plan

1. **Define your current and future financial goals.** Any successful financial plan incorporates both long-term goals, like owning a second vacation home or putting all of your kids through college, and short-term goals, such as the amount of money you need

to pay your monthly bills. Listing these goals at the beginning of your investment plan will help you structure the plan to meet your needs today and ensure you'll reach your goals tomorrow.

2. **Identify a timeframe for achieving your goals.** It's fine and good to determine the lifestyle you want to have someday upon retirement, but if you don't specifically define what you mean by "someday," you're in danger of creating an investment portfolio that won't meet your long-term goals. As we discussed in Leg Two of this book, you must design your portfolio to include the right mix of assets that will minimize risk while maximizing returns. This mix is inextricably tied to your retirement time horizon and will vary according to whether you want to retire in 5, 10, or 15 years—or longer.

3. **Decide on an acceptable rate of return.** Some investors do their due diligence by establishing their investment goals and time horizon, yet they still end up shocked when they receive their first portfolio statement. That's because these investors likely didn't think about how their goals and timeframe would translate into regular rates of return—which can be disarming for those who plan to retire later and therefore assume more short-term risk to achieve larger long-term gains. Be sure your advisor spells out the types of return rates you can expect based on your goals and time horizon; if you find you're uncomfortable with these rates, your advisor can help you to tweak your plan so it strikes a good balance between your goals and rate-of-return comfort level.

4. **Outline a specific strategy for asset allocation.** From reading this book, you already know how important it is to structure your investment portfolio around the idea of asset allocation. The mix of asset classes in your portfolio contributes to the rate of return I discussed in step 3 above, so it's critical for your advisor to get

specific about the types and quantities of assets she or he plans to include in that portfolio. Be sure your plan includes precise details about the combination of the three main asset classes—which you probably remember are cash/money markets, bonds, and stocks—you can expect to see in your regular statements. This will prevent ambiguity and provide you and your advisor with a reference point should questions arise later.

5. **Determine methods for monitoring your portfolio.** At this point, you've finished building a solid foundation for your investment plan. But as I mentioned under part one, changing circumstances can throw a wrench into even the most well-crafted plan. It's imperative, then, that your personal investment plan include rules for regular monitoring of your portfolio's performance by your advisor. This entails defining the benchmarks your advisor will measure your portfolio against, as well as establishing how often your advisor will review your investments. Though the two of you already established a schedule for how often you'll meet, a good advisor will want to review your plan more frequently than right before your meetings, and proactively contact you should he discover issues that must be discussed.

Rodgers' Recommendations for Writing a Personal Financial Plan

- Writing a personal financial plan helps you define the financial position you hope to be in upon retirement, and provides guidance for the advisor you'll work with to get there.

- You should write your personal financial plan in two parts. Part one revolves around the terms of communication you can expect from your advisor; part two includes specifics about how your advisor will allocate your assets and monitor your portfolio's success.

- Make your plan as specific as possible, incorporating precise details wherever you can. The more specificity you include, the less room for confusion—and the better chance for good investment returns.

Glossary

ADV part II
A form that is similar to a prospectus on an advisory firm, explaining potential conflicts of interest

AIME
Average indexed monthly earnings

Amortization
The process of decreasing or accounting for an amount over a period of time

Annuitization
The process of taking an asset and, by way of an installment sale or annuity sale, effectively converting the asset into a stream of payments

Annuity factor
Another phrase for the life-expectancy factor

BB corporate bond
A type of high-yield bond

CD
Certificate of deposit

Crummey letters
A term taken from the case Crummey vs. Commissioner, which defined the process of having beneficiaries of estate gifts sign a

letter stating they've been given the opportunity to withdraw the gift within the 30-day withdrawal-rights period and have chosen to decline the right

CRUT
Charitable remainder unitrust

DALBAR
A firm that develops standards for—and provides research, ratings, and rankings of intangible factors to—the financial services industry

Efficient frontier
The combinations of investments exhibiting the optimal risk/ reward trade-off

ERISA
Employee retirement income security act

FICA
Payroll taxes

FUTA
Federal unemployment tax

GRAT
Grantor retained annuity trust

ILIT
Irrevocable life insurance trust

Junk bond
A type of high-yield bond

MAGI
Modified adjusted gross income

NAV
Net asset value

OASDI
Old age survivor and disability insurance

PIA
Primary insurance amount

RBD
Required beginning date

R/D factor
The retirement distribution factor, a scale from 0 (the point at which all of your income is taxable) to 100 (where all of your retirement income is tax-free) against which you can measure how well you've done with reducing your taxable retirement income by building a balanced three-legged stool

SPD
Summary plan description

SSI
Social security

About Rick Rodgers

Rick Rodgers earned the prestigious Certified Financial Planner™ (CFP®) designation in 1999. To become a CFP® professional, he successfully completed a comprehensive course of study culminating in a 10-hour, two-day test, proving his understanding of financial planning, tax planning, employee benefits, retirement planning, estate planning, investment management, and asset protection.

Rick began his career as a financial advisor with Shearson Lehman Brothers in 1984, working as a financial consultant and qualified plans coordinator until joining Prudential Securities in 1990. At Prudential, he received regular promotions and achieved the level of First Vice President—Investments. In 1996, he left Prudential to found Rodgers & Associates, in order to help families create and conserve their wealth in preparation for worry-free and dignified retirements. With a commitment to help his clients plan for the future while living in the present, Rick offers an individually focused approach to helping clients reach their retirement goals.

Rick continually strives to help his clients though his common sense investment approach. With 25 years of experience in the financial services industry, Rick's knowledge and experience were further rewarded when he became one of the first advisors to receive the Certified Retirement Counselor® (CRC®) designation from the International Foundation for Retirement Education. His commitment to the retirement market is further evidenced by the awarding of the Chartered Retirement Planning Counselor SM designation.

In July 2007, for the fifth consecutive year, *Wealth Manager* magazine named Rodgers & Associates one of the country's top wealth managers. *Wealth Manager* magazine's ranking of Top Wealth Managers is based on the asset value of each participating wealth manager's average client relationships as of December 31, 2006, and is calculated by dividing the total assets under management by the total number of client relationships. Rodgers & Associates was one of only four firms named from Central Pennsylvania, ranking 401 of 464 wealth managers.

Rodgers is past president and a founder of the CPA Advantage of Lancaster and a 1987 graduate of Leadership Lancaster. He also served as a field representative for the Northeast to Larry Burkett's organization, Christian Financial Concepts, from 1990 to 1995. He is a current member of the prestigious National Association of Personal Financial Advisors (NAPFA) and the Financial Planning Association; served on the TD Ameritrade 2006-2007 Board of Advisors and on the finance committee of the local United Way; and is a member of the Board of The James Buchanan Foundation.

Rodgers can be reached via email at rick@rodgers-associates.com or by telephone at 717-560-3800.

Free 2 Week Trial Offer for U.S. Residents From Investor's Business Daily:

FREE 2 WEEK Trial Offer

INVESTOR'S BUSINESS DAILY will provide you with the facts, figures, and objective news analysis you need to succeed.

Investor's Business Daily is formatted for a quick and concise read to help you make informed and profitable decisions.

To take advantage of this free 2 week trial offer, e-mail us at customerservice@fpbooks.com or visit our website at www.fpbooks.com where you find other free offers as well.

You can also reach us by calling 800-272-2855.

This book, along with other books, is available at discounts that make it realistic to provide it as a gift to your customers, clients, and staff. For more information on these long lasting, cost effective premiums, please call us at (800) 272-2855 or you may email us at sales@fpbooks.com.